Brilliant Excel
VBA Programming

Curtis Frye

PEARSON

Harlow, England • London • New York • Boston • San Francisco • Toronto • Sydney • Auckland • Singapore • Hong Kong
Tokyo • Seoul • Taipei • New Delhi • Cape Town • São Paulo • Mexico City • Madrid • Amsterdam • Munich • Paris • Milan

PEARSON EDUCATION LIMITED

Edinburgh Gate
Harlow CM20 2JE
United Kingdom
Tel: +44 (0)1279 623623
Web: www.pearson.com/uk

First published 2013 (print and electronic)

Pearson Education is not responsible for the content of third-party Internet sites.

ISBN: 978-0-273-77197-5 (print)
    978-0-273-77290-3 (PDF)
    978-0-273-77289-7 (ePub)

British Library Cataloguing-in-Publication Data
A catalogue record for the print edition is available from the British Library

Library of Congress Cataloging-in-Publication Data
Frye, Curtis, 1968-
  Brilliant Excel VBA programming / Curtis Frye.
    pages cm. -- (Brilliant guides)
  ISBN 978-0-273-77197-5 (limp)
  1. Microsoft Excel (Computer file) 2. Microsoft Visual Basic for applications. 3. Business--Computer programs. 4. Electronic spreadsheets spreadsheets. I. Title.
  HF5548.4.M523F782 2013
  005.54--dc23
                    2012049451

The screenshots in this book are reprinted by permission of Microsoft Corporation.

ARP Impression 98

Print edition typeset in 11/14pt Arial MT Std Condensed by 30
Printed by Ashford Colour Press Ltd.

NOTE THAT ANY PAGE CROSS-REFERENCES REFER TO THE PRINT EDITION

Brilliant guides

What you need to know and how to do it

When you're working on your computer and come up against a problem that you're unsure how to solve, or want to accomplish something in an application that you aren't sure how to do, where do you look? Manuals and traditional training guides are usually too big and unwieldy and are intended to be used as end-to-end training resources, making it hard to get to the info you need right away without having to wade through pages of background information that you just don't need at that moment – and helplines are rarely that helpful!

Brilliant guides have been developed to allow you to find the info you need easily and without fuss and guide you through the task using a highly visual, step-by-step approach – providing exactly what you need to know when you need it!

Brilliant guides provide the quick easy-to-access information that you need, using a table of contents and troubleshooting guide to help you find exactly what you need to know, and then presenting each task in a visual manner. Numbered steps guide you through each task or problem, using numerous screenshots to illustrate each step. Added features include 'See also...' boxes that point you to related tasks and information in the book, while 'Did you know?...' sections alert you to relevant expert tips, tricks and advice to further expand your skills and knowledge.

In addition to covering all major office PC applications, and related computing subjects, the *Brilliant* series also contains titles that will help you in every aspect of your working life, such as writing the perfect CV, answering the toughest interview questions and moving on in your career.

Brilliant guides are the light at the end of the tunnel when you are faced with any minor or major task.

Author's acknowledgements

No book is a singular effort. I'm grateful to Joli Ballew, a long-time Pearson author, and my agent Neil Salkind of The Salkind Agency and Studio B for inviting me to take on this project. I'd also like to thank Robert Cottee and Steve Temblett of Pearson UK for their help managing the project, Helen Savill for her editorial guidance and all members of the production team who copy edited, proofread and produced the finished work. I know the amount of work that goes into producing a book after the writing is done and appreciate their efforts.

About the author

Curtis Frye is the author of more than two dozen books, including *Microsoft Excel 2013 Step by Step* for Microsoft Press and the *Excel 2007 Pocket Guide* for O'Reilly Media. He has also written and hosted over a dozen online training courses on Excel and other programs for lynda.com. In addition to his writing, Curt is a popular keynote speaker and has performed with the ComedySportz Portland improv comedy group since 1996. He lives in Portland, Oregon, with his wife Virginia, their three cats and many, many books.

Dedication

For Colin and Emily

Contents

Introduction

Welcome to *Brilliant Excel VBA Programming*, a visual quick reference book that shows you how to use VBA programming to import data and produce reports more efficiently in Excel. This book provides complete coverage of basic to advanced VBA programming skills.

Find what you need to know – when you need it

You don't have to read this book in any particular order. We've designed the book so that you can jump in, get the information you need and jump out. To find the information that you need, just look up the task in the table of contents or Troubleshooting guide, and turn to the page listed. Read the task introduction, follow the step-by-step instructions along with the illustration, and you're done.

How this book works

Each task is presented with step-by-step instructions in one column and screen illustrations in the other. This arrangement lets you focus on a single task without having to turn the pages too often.

What you'll do

Find what you need to know – when you need it

How this book works

Step-by-step instructions

Troubleshooting guide

Spelling

Step-by-step instructions

This book provides concise step-by-step instructions that show you how to accomplish a task. Each set of instructions includes illustrations that directly correspond to the easy-to-read steps. Eye-catching text features provide additional helpful information in bite-sized chunks to help you work more efficiently or to teach you more in-depth information. The 'For your information' features provide tips and techniques to help you work smarter, while the 'See also' cross-references lead you to other parts of the book containing related information about the task. Essential information is highlighted in 'Important' boxes that will ensure you don't miss any vital suggestions and advice.

Troubleshooting guide

This book offers quick and easy ways to diagnose and solve common problems that you might encounter, using the Troubleshooting guide. The problems are grouped into categories that are presented alphabetically.

Spelling

We have used UK spelling conventions throughout this book. You may therefore notice some inconsistencies between the text and the software on your computer, which is likely to have been developed in the US. We have, however, adopted US spelling for the words 'disk' and 'program', as these are commonly accepted throughout the world.

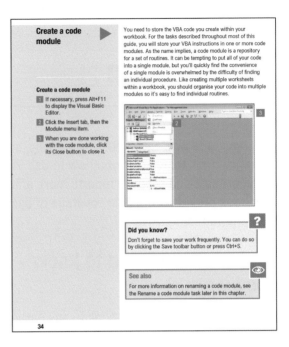

Recording and running macros

Introduction

Macros are sets of recorded instructions you can replay whenever you wish. If you perform a multi-step task frequently, such as applying formats to an Excel worksheet, you could record the steps as a macro. Then, the next time you want to perform those actions, you can save yourself a lot of time by running the macro. You can choose from several options for running your macros, depending on whether you want to use your keyboard, click a shape, run your macro from the Macros dialog box or add a button to the Quick Access Toolbar. Finally, you'll learn how to manage macro security in Excel 2010.

What you'll do

Record a macro

Run a macro

Edit a macro

Delete a macro

Record a macro using relative references

Assign a macro to a keyboard shortcut

Run a macro by clicking a shape

Add a macro to the Quick Access Toolbar

Customise a Quick Access Toolbar button

Save a macro-enabled workbook

Managing Excel 2010 security settings

Change Protected View settings

Change message bar settings

Change data connection security settings

Add a digital signature to a workbook

Record a macro

Macros are sets of steps that you can replay with the click of a button or press of a key. Before you can replay those steps, however, you must record them. When you start recording, everything you do is stored in the macro. If you make a mistake, you can stop recording, return your worksheet to its original configuration and try again. Once your macro is in place, you can run it any time you wish and have the steps completed almost instantly.

To start recording a macro, display the View tab on the ribbon, then follow the steps.

Record a macro

1 Click the View tab.

2 Click the Macros button's down arrow.

3 Click Record Macro.

4 In the Record Macro dialog box, type a name for your macro.

5 Click OK.

6 Perform the steps you would like to record and play back later.

7 Click View, click the Macros button's down arrow and click Stop Recording.

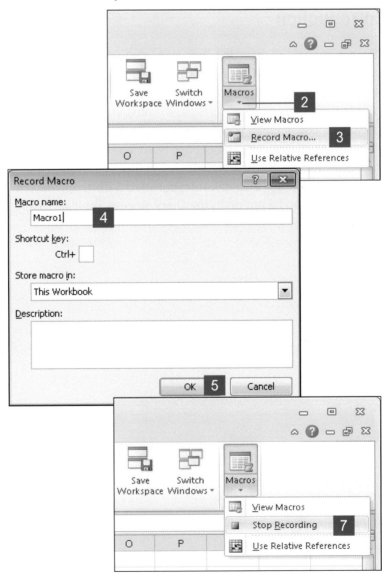

After you record a macro, running it replays those steps in just a few seconds. For example, suppose you copy customer orders from one worksheet to another. If doing so takes you a minute to complete and you do it once a day, you'll save 20 minutes per month on that task alone by creating a macro.

You'll find the controls to run a macro via the Excel user interface on the View tab.

Run a macro

1 Click the View tab.

2 Click Macros, to display the Macro dialog box.

3 Click the macro you want to run.

4 Click Run.

Important

Click the main body of the Macros button on the ribbon to display the Macro dialog box.

See also

If you display multiple worksheets while recording a macro, your screen might flicker. For information on how to stop the screen from flickering, see Chapter 11.

Edit a macro

After you have recorded a macro, you might find that you want to change one of its steps. For example, instead of changing the text to red, you might want to display it in blue. Rather than record a new macro and delete the old, you can save time by editing your existing macro.

Edit a macro

1 Click the View tab.

2 Click Macros.

3 In the Macro dialog box, click the macro you want to change.

4 Click Edit.

```
Sub FormatSalesInfo()
'
' FormatSalesInfo Macro
'

        Selection.Font.Italic = True
        Selection.Font.Bold = True
End Sub
```

5 With the macro open in the Visual Basic Editor, change the code in the code module.

6 Click the Save button on the toolbar.

7 Click File…Close and Return to Microsoft Excel on the menu.

Did you know?

If you're not sure if your edit will make your macro inoperable, copy the text you're changing to a text file or e-mail message so you can paste it back in if needed.

Jargon buster

When you record a macro, Excel writes the Visual Basic for Applications instructions required to duplicate your steps. Those instructions are stored in a **code module**, which you'll learn more about in Chapter 2.

Delete a macro

If you're done with a macro and don't anticipate using it again, you can delete it from your workbook. Deleting unwanted macros makes the list that appears in the Macro dialog box less crowded, which, in turn, makes it easier for you to find the macro you want to run.

Delete a macro

1 Display the macros in your workbook by clicking the View tab.

2 Click Macros.

3 In the Macro dialog box, click the macro you want to delete.

4 Click Delete.

5 Click Yes to confirm you want to delete the macro.

! Important

Deleting a macro is final – once you do, you can't bring it back.

? Did you know?

If you've had a change of heart, click No to leave the macro in your workbook.

When you create a macro, Excel makes a note of the exact cells you selected when you recorded your macro's steps. If you click cell C3 and then C4 (the cell below C3), the macro code will contain those exact cell references. If you would rather your macro code indicate that you clicked the cell just below the active cell, rather than a specific cell address, you can record your macro using relative references.

Jargon buster

A **relative reference** is an instruction that tells Excel to look a number of rows up or down and a number of columns to the left or right of the active cell.

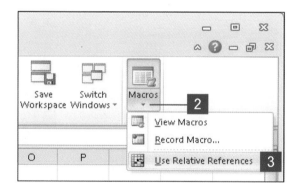

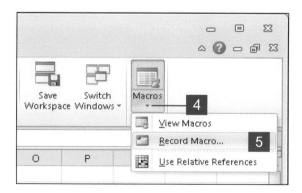

Record a macro using relative references

1 Indicate you want to do this by clicking the View tab.

2 Click the Macros button's down arrow.

3 Click Use Relative References.

4 Now you can record the macro normally – click the Macros button's down arrow.

5 Click Record Macro to display the Macro dialog box.

Record a macro using relative references (cont.)

6 In the Record Macro dialog box, type a name for your macro.

7 Click OK.

8 Perform the steps you want to record.

9 Click the View tab.

10 Click the Macros button's down arrow.

11 Click Stop Recording. Play back later.

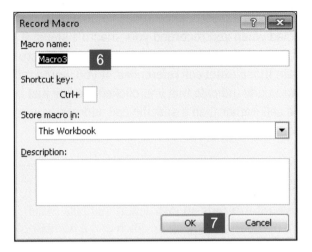

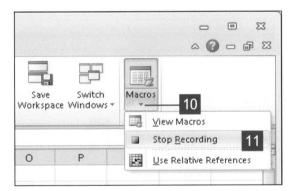

Important

If your macro doesn't behave the way you expect, click View and then click the Macros button's down arrow to see if Use Relative References is highlighted.

If you run a macro frequently, you might want to assign it to a keyboard shortcut. Just as you can press Ctrl+C to copy a cell's contents in Excel, you can have Excel run a macro whenever you press a certain key combination. You must use a letter, so you should assign rarely used letters such as J, M or U to your macros.

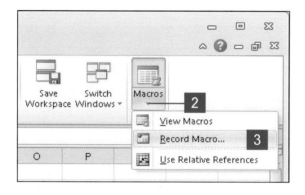

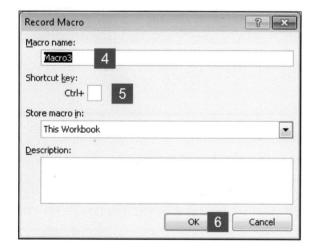

Assign a macro to a keyboard shortcut

Assign a macro to a keyboard shortcut

1 Click the View tab to start the macro recording process.

2 Click the Macros button's down arrow.

3 Click Record Macro.

4 In the Macro dialog box, type a name for your macro.

5 In the Shortcut key box, type a letter to be pressed with the Ctrl key to run the macro.

6 Click OK.

Assign a macro to a keyboard shortcut (cont.)

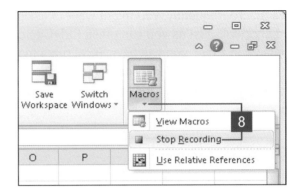

7 Perform the steps you want to record.

8 On the ribbon, click View, click the Macros button's down arrow, then click Stop Recording. Play back later.

!

Important

If you assign a macro to a common keyboard shortcut, such as Ctrl+C (which copies the selected cells' contents), then pressing that key sequence while editing the workbook will run the macro *instead of* performing the shortcut's usual function.

?

Did you know?

You can assign a keyboard shortcut to a macro after you create it by opening the Macro dialog box, clicking the macro, clicking the Options button, then typing the keyboard shortcut into the Shortcut key box.

If you create macros for several different workbooks, it can be difficult to remember which macros are available where. Rather than take the time to open the Macro dialog box to discover which macros are contained in a workbook, you can make your macros more visible by assigning them to a shape and editing the shape's text to reflect the macro. Then, when you click the shape, Excel runs the macro.

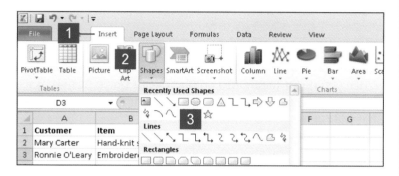

Run a macro by clicking a shape

1 Click the Insert tab.

2 Click Shapes.

3 Click the type of shape you want to add.

4 Draw the shape in the body of your worksheet.

5 If desired, click the shape and type text to appear in the shape as a label.

6 Right-click the shape and then click Assign Macro.

7 In the Assign Macro dialog box, click the macro you want to run when the shape is clicked.

8 Click OK.

Did you know?

In addition to shapes, you can also assign macros to pictures and clip art.

Did you know?

To select a shape, picture or clip art image rather than run a macro assigned to it, hold down the Ctrl key when you click the object.

Add a macro to the Quick Access Toolbar

If you record a macro that you use frequently, you should consider assigning the macro to a button you add to the Quick Access Toolbar. You can find the Quick Access Toolbar above the ribbon. When you install Excel, the Quick Access Toolbar contains the Save, Undo and Redo buttons. Assigning a macro to a Quick Access Tollbar. button lets you run the macro easily — all you need to do is click the button you created.

Add a macro to the Quick Access Toolbar

1 Right-click any blank spot on the ribbon and then click Customize Quick Access Toolbar....

2 In the Excel Options dialog box, click the Choose commands from down arrow and then click Macros.

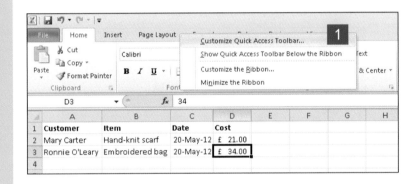

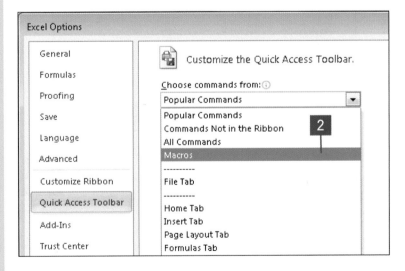

Did you know?

You can change the order of buttons on the Quick Access Toolbar by displaying the Quick Access Toolbar page of the Excel Options dialog box, clicking the name of the macro you want to reposition and clicking the Move Up and Move Down buttons at the right edge of the dialog box.

3 In the left-hand pane, click the macro you want to add to the Quick Access Toolbar.

4 Click the Add button.

5 Click OK. When you do, a button representing the macro appears on the Quick Access Toolbar.

Customise a Quick Access Toolbar button

When you add a macro to the Quick Access Toolbar, Excel assigns it a button that looks like a miniature flowchart. It's an appropriate image, but if you have multiple macros on the Quick Access Toolbar you won't be able to tell them apart at a glance. You can always hover the mouse pointer over a button to see which macro it runs, but it's far easier to change the button's image so it stands out on the Quick Access Toolbar.

Customise a Quick Access Toolbar button

1 Right-click any blank spot on the ribbon and then click Customize Quick Access Toolbar.

Did you know?

When you hover the mouse pointer over a Quick Access Toolbar button, Excel displays the name of the macro that will run when the button is clicked. You can change that text by changing the Display Name value in the Modify Button dialog box. Click the macro you want to customise and then click the Modify button.

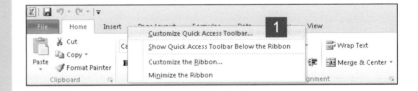

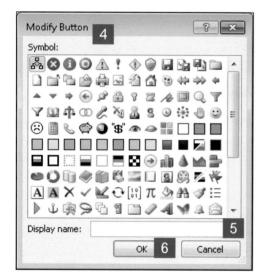

2 In the Customize Quick Access Toolbar panel of the Excel Options dialog box, click the macro you want to assign a new button image to.

3 Click Modify.

4 In the Modify Button dialog box, click a new button image.

5 If desired, in the Display name box, type a new name to appear when you hover the mouse pointer over the button.

6 Click OK.

7 Click OK.

Did you know?

To delete a Quick Access Toolbar button, display the Quick Access Toolbar page of the Excel Options dialog box, click the macro you want to remove, click the Remove button, then click OK.

Save a macro-enabled workbook

For security reasons, Excel 2010 doesn't let you save a workbook with macros using the standard .xlsx file type. Instead, you must save the file as a macro-enabled workbook. Windows Explorer displays these files with a different icon so it's very easy to tell that a file contains code that could run when you open it.

Save a macro-enabled workbook

1 Click the File tab on the ribbon.

2 Click Save As.

3 In the Save As dialog box, type a name for the workbook in the File name box.

4 Click the Save as type control's down arrow, then click Excel Macro-Enabled Workbook and click Save.

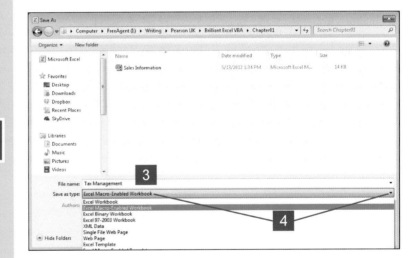

Important !

Avoid opening macro-enabled files you didn't expect to receive and always keep your antivirus software up to date.

Excel 2003 and earlier versions of Excel had relatively unsophisticated macro security measures in place, so it was fairly easy for malicious programmers to create *macro viruses* (harmful computer code written using VBA) to spread malware via infected files. Starting with Excel 2007 and continuing in Excel 2010, the Office programming team instituted much stricter controls over when and how macros may be used. Disallowing macros in the default file format has gone a long way towards securing Excel against malicious code. Even so, it is still possible for users to inadvertently open an infected macro-enabled file, so it is best that you acquire reputable virus protection software and set your macro security settings at the highest level that makes sense for your operation.

Changing macro security settings

Excel 2010 gives you a lot of control over the program's security settings. Macros written by malicious coders can do significant damage to your computer and its data, so it makes sense to apply stringent security settings. You have several options from which to choose – you should select the one that provides the most security without compromising your operations.

The most restrictive macro security choice is to disable all macros without notification. Selecting this setting means that Excel prohibits all macros, regardless of any other security features, such as digital signatures, applied to the macros. As this is a book about writing VBA code, you most likely won't be surprised that this is not the recommended setting for your macro security. That said, if you are not currently working with macro-enabled workbooks and do not expect to receive any such files, you should strongly consider adopting this security setting, at least temporarily.

Manage Excel 2010 security settings

1

Change macro security settings

1 Click the File tab.

2 Click Options.

Manage Excel 2010 security settings (cont.)

3 In the Excel Options dialog box, click Trust Center.

4 Click Trust Center Settings.

5 Click Macro Settings.

6 Select the option for the level of macro security you want apply. Note that you can:

   a. Disable all macros without notification.

   b. Disable all macros with notification.

   c. Disable all macros except digitally signed macros.

   d. Enable all macros.

7 Click OK twice to finalise your changes.

The next setting, disable all macros with notification, protects against macros by default, but displays an alert on the message bar indicating that the file contains macros. If you wish, you may click the Enable Content button to run macros while you have the workbook open. If you expect to work with macro-enabled workbooks frequently, this is a good setting to choose. You can also choose to disable all macros except digitally signed ones. Digital signatures (described later in this chapter) are constructs that provide an extra layer of security to digital files. If you expect to receive macros from known publishers that use digital signatures to authenticate their work, you should choose this setting.

Finally, you could choose to enable all macros. Doing so is not recommended. Even though malware protection software is substantially more effective than it used to be, it won't catch everything. Your best course of action is to select a setting that disables at least some macros by default and lets you decide whether or not to allow them to run.

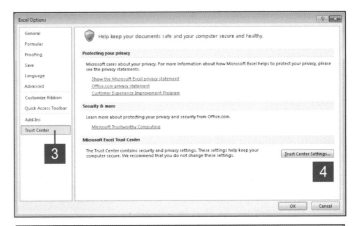

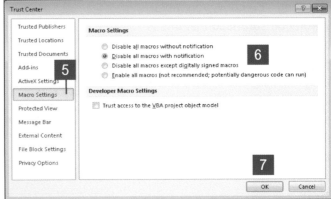

When you receive a file by e-mail or download it from the Internet, Office 2010 programs can open the file in what is called Protected View. As the name implies, Protected View is a mode that prevents any sort of active content, such as ActiveX controls or macros, from running on your computer. You can select from several options to enhance your security using Protected View.

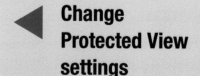

Change Protected View settings

Change Protected View settings

1 Click the File tab.

2 Click Options.

3 Click Trust Center.

4 Click Trust Center Settings.

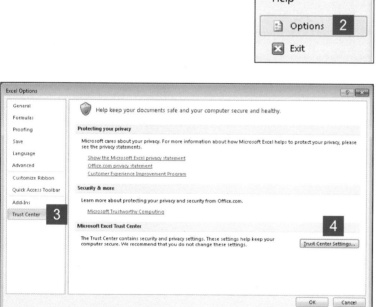

Change Protected View settings (cont.)

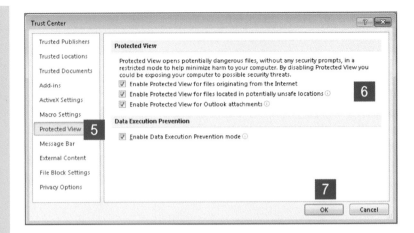

5 Click Protected View in the left-hand panel.

6 Select the Protected View options you want to enable. Note that you can:

a. Enable Protected View for files originating from the Internet.

b. Enable Protected View for files located in potentially unsafe locations.

c. Enable Protected View for Outlook attachments.

d. Enable Data Execution Prevention mode.

7 Click OK twice to finalise your changes.

Important

By default, all of the Protected View settings are switched on when you install Office 2010. Unless there is a very good reason to do so, you should not alter any of these settings.

Many very useful workbooks contain macros that extend the functionality of Excel 2010. Even so, you might find that your macro security settings prohibit your code from running when you desire. Even if your settings disable macros by default, you can have Excel display a message bar indicating that it has detected macros in your workbook and the action it has taken. Based on your other security settings, you can then either acknowledge the message and turn on macros or close the message bar without allowing macros to run.

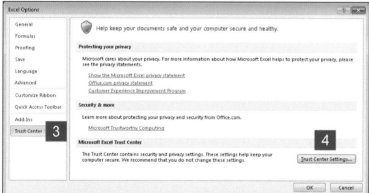

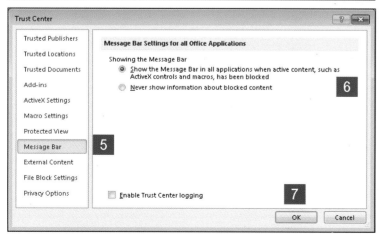

Change message bar settings

Change message bar settings

1 To display the Excel Options dialog box, click the File tab.

2 Click Options.

3 Click Trust Center.

4 Click Trust Center Settings.

5 Click Message Bar.

6 Select the option you want to apply to the Message Bar. Note that you can:

a. Show the Message Bar when active content is blocked.

b. Never show information about blocked content.

7 Click OK twice to finalise your changes.

Did you know?

You can hide the message bar by clicking the Close button, which looks like a small letter 'X', at the far right edge of the bar.

Change data connection security settings

If your organisation is large enough that you store data in several different repositories, you will most likely bring that data into Excel using a data connection or a workbook link. *Data connections* are connections to other data sources, such as SQL databases, which can introduce their own security issues. *Workbook links* are connections to other Excel files. This latter type of connection has become much more common now that Excel workbooks can contain over a million rows of data per worksheet.

Change data connection security settings

1 Open the Excel Options dialog box by clicking the File tab.

2 Click Options.

3 Click Trust Center.

4 Click Trust Center Settings.

As with many of the other security settings in this section, you can choose to enable data connections or workbook links, prompt users to choose whether to update the connections or links or else disable connections and links entirely. The most common setting is to prompt users to choose whether to update or not. This setting alerts you that your workbook contains one of those two elements. If you're expecting a workbook to contain a data connection or workbook link, you can allow Excel to make the connection. If, however, you receive a file that you did not expect to contain either of those two elements, you can choose not to enable them and check with the individual who sent it to you or your corporate IT professional to determine the best course of action.

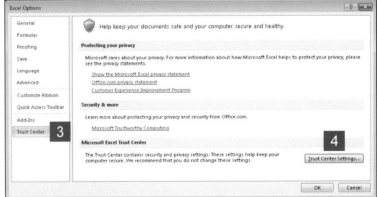

Change data connection security settings (cont.)

1

5 Click External Content.

6 Select the Security settings for Data Connections. You can:

  a. Enable all Data Connections.

  b. Prompt user about Data Connections.

  c. Disable all Data Connections.

7 Select the Security settings for Workbook Links. You can:

  a. Enable automatic link updates.

  b. Prompt users on automatic update for Workbook Links.

  c. Disable automatic update of Workbook Links.

8 Click OK twice to finalise your changes.

Add a digital signature to a workbook

As mentioned earlier in this chapter, one of the macro security settings for Excel 2010 is to allow only those macros that have a *digital signature* attached. A digital signature is a file, generated by a certification authority, that Excel can use to identify a document as having been created by the certificate owner. You can purchase several different levels of digital certificate, based on the extent of the documentation you provide to the certifying authority.

Add a digital signature to a workbook

1 Click the File tab.

2 If necessary, click Info.

3 Click Protect Workbook.

4 Click Add a Digital Signature.

5 Click OK.

Did you know?

You can get more information about digital certificates by clicking the Signature Services from the Office Marketplace button that appears after you click the Add a Digital Signature button.

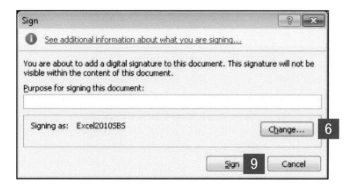

6 Click Change...

7 Click the digital signature you want to use.

8 Click OK.

9 Click Sign to add the digital signature to your workbook.

?

Did you know?

For more information on managing publishers with digital certificates, click the File tab, click Options, click Trust Center, click Trust Center Settings, then click Trusted Publishers.

Starting with the Visual Basic Editor

2

Introduction

Microsoft Excel provides an ideal environment for examining numerical data, especially that of the financial variety. You could use Microsoft Word tables to summarise your data and even to perform some simple calculations, but it is by far the inferior tool. If you or a colleague develop web pages, you know that it's possible to create a page using a simple text editor such as Notepad. Possible, but certainly much more difficult than necessary.

Just as you could create a web page using nothing but a simple text editor, it's possible to create your VBA code in Notepad. Possible, but difficult. The best tool for the job, the Visual Basic Editor, is built into the Microsoft office application suite. You can display the Visual Basic Editor using a single key sequence and use its considerable power to create, edit and manage your VBA code.

In this chapter, you will learn how to work with the Visual Basic Editor, create simple code constructs, such as subroutines and functions, and save your work to a text file.

What you'll do

Introduce object-orientated programming

Display the Developer ribbon tab

Display the Visual Basic Editor

Set project properties

Create a code module

Create a subroutine

Create a function

Add a comment to your code

Run a VBA routine

Rename a code module

Delete a code module

Export a code module to a text file

Introduce object-orientated programming

When you write or record a VBA macro in Excel, you define a set of instructions for the program to follow. Computers take your instructions absolutely literally, meaning that they will do exactly what you tell them to do, even if that is not what you mean for them to do. Every programming language follows a well-defined set of patterns to reduce ambiguity, but the best programming languages combine power, flexibility and the ability for humans to comprehend the instructions.

Early generations of programming languages were called *procedural languages*, which allowed programmers to define a series of steps called an *algorithm*. The code in the algorithm manipulated *variables*, which contain values used in calculations and other manipulations. The great insight of *object-orientated programming* – which is a means of organising knowledge about a particular domain – was that a programming environment referred to things. For example, in Excel you have workbooks, worksheets, cells, charts and a myriad of other objects to which you can refer.

Procedural programming languages also enabled programmers to refer to objects by using what were called *abstract data types*. You could define an abstract data type, perhaps a product offered by a company, then create instances of those abstract data types. For example, you could create an instance of the product data type to refer to an automobile, a hotel room or a computer.

Abstract data types offered procedural programming languages extra capabilities, but they were a bit of a haphazard addition to the underlying language. So, language designers extended the concept of the abstract data type and organised their languages by defining every element of the programming domain as an *object*. Each object, in turn, has a number of elements encapsulated within it. There are three elements you can find within Microsoft Excel objects in Excel VBA:

- properties
- methods
- events.

Objects may also be members of *collections*, which are groups of like objects. For example, the set of all worksheets within a workbook is called the Worksheets collection.

Properties

As the name implies, properties are some aspect of an object. For example, a workbook has a name, a collection of worksheets and information about the date it was created. You can change most of these values using the file system, such as by renaming a workbook, or VBA code. Some properties are set by the system and can't be manipulated directly, but you can read them if you need to use the information they contain. You refer to properties using what is called *dot notation*. As an example, you would refer to the name of the first worksheet in a workbook using the code `Worksheet(1).Name`.

Methods

Properties describe some aspect of an object – they are the adjectives that modify the object's noun. Methods represent action verbs – specifically, actions that the object knows how to take. For example, you can save the current state of your workbook, change worksheets within the workbook, or delete a worksheet using methods that are built into the Excel object model. You also refer to an object's methods using dot notation. For example, you could change the active worksheet by using the code `Worksheet(Name).Activate`.

Events

If methods are the action verbs of the object-orientated programming world, then events are the passive verbs. An event is something that happens to an object inside an object-orientated programming language. Excel 2010 can recognise many different events, some of which are:

■ opening or closing of a workbook

■ activating or deactivating a worksheet

■ saving a workbook

■ clicking a chart

Introduce object-orientated programming (cont.)

- adding data to a cell
- recalculating a worksheet
- following a hyperlink.

As soon as Excel recognises one of these events has happened, it triggers an event handler that executes any code you have written within it. Events are extremely powerful, but it is very easy to run into trouble by creating a series of event handlers that could potentially trigger each other. The resulting chain reaction will render Excel useless until you halt the program's execution by pressing Ctrl+C.

If you plan to do a lot of programming work in Excel 2010, you should take a moment to add the built-in Developer tab to the ribbon user interface. The Developer tab contains many tools that you would normally find under separate ribbon tabs in the standard user interface. For example, you can display the Visual Basic Editor, record a macro, indicate you want to use relative references in a macro, or change macro security settings by clicking a single ribbon control.

 Display the Developer ribbon tab

Display the Developer ribbon tab

1 Open the Excel Options dialog box by clicking the File tab, then Options.

2 In the Excel Options dialog box, click Customize Ribbon.

3 If necessary, click the Customize the Ribbon down arrow and click Main Tabs.

4 Click the Developer box.

5 Click OK.

Important

If your keyboard doesn't have working function keys or if for some reason either your Alt or F11 keys aren't working properly, you should display the Developer tab so you can click the Visual Basic control to display the Visual Basic Editor without using the keyboard.

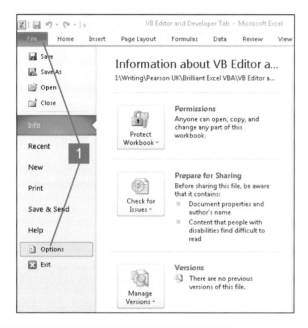

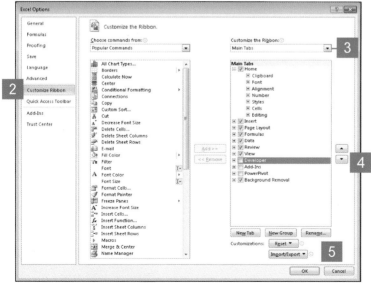

Display the Visual Basic Editor

Excel, like the other Microsoft Office programs, includes the Visual Basic Editor. The Visual Basic Editor is a dedicated tool you can use to write your VBA routines, edit existing macros and create functions that let you perform calculations using customised procedures that you define.

Display the Visual Basic Editor

1 Either:

  a. Press Alt+F11.

  b. Click the Developer tab, then Visual Basic.

2 When you are done working in the Visual Basic Editor, Click the File...Close and Return to Microsoft Excel menu item.

Did you know?

After you open the Visual Basic Editor, pressing Alt+F11 enables you to switch between Excel and the Visual Basic Editor without closing either.

See also

For information on displaying the Developer ribbon tab, see the Displaying the Developer ribbon tab task from earlier in this chapter.

Each workbook will have its own VBA project associated with it. In turn, every VBA project has a name. The names Excel provides are neutral and, frankly, uninformative. You can change the value of the project's name property to clarify the workbook's purpose.

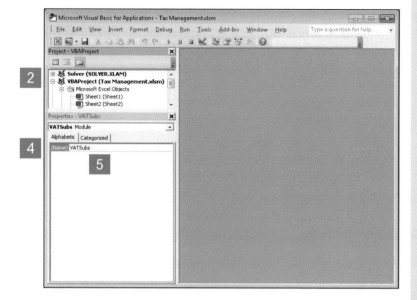

Set project properties

Set project properties

1 Press Alt+F11 to display the Visual Basic Editor.

2 In the Project panel, click VBAProject.

3 If necessary, click the View... Properties Window menu item to activate the Properties panel.

4 Click the property you want to modify.

5 Type a new value for the property.

Did you know?

Adding a few characters to a project name can help identify which file and program it belongs to. For example, you could name a project Payroll_wbk to indicate it's an Excel workbook. Useful abbreviations include _doc for Word documents and _ppt for PowerPoint presentations.

Create a code module

Create a code module

1. If necessary, press Alt+F11 to display the Visual Basic Editor.

2. Click the Insert tab, then the Module menu item.

3. When you are done working with the code module, click its Close button to close it.

You need to store the VBA code you create within your workbook. For the tasks described throughout most of this guide, you will store your VBA instructions in one or more code modules. As the name implies, a code module is a repository for a set of routines. It can be tempting to put all of your code into a single module, but you'll quickly find the convenience of a single module is overwhelmed by the difficulty of finding an individual procedure. Like creating multiple worksheets within a workbook, you should organise your code into multiple modules so it's easy to find individual routines.

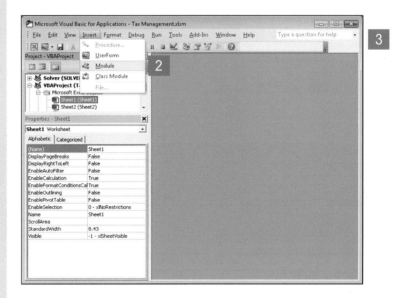

Did you know?

Don't forget to save your work frequently. You can do so by clicking the Save toolbar button or press Ctrl+S.

See also

For more information on renaming a code module, see the Rename a code module task later in this chapter.

The most common type of VBA routine you will write is called a subroutine. A *subroutine* is a series of instructions that can affect workbooks or their contents but doesn't return a value that you can use in a formula. For example, if your subroutine is named DisplayVAT, you could display the value in a message box but not create a formula such as =DisplayVAT(A1). Despite that limitation, subroutines are enormously useful and will figure prominently in your VBA work.

In the task, the word 'Sub' in the code is the keyword identifying your code as a subroutine, the name is the name of the subroutine, which must be unique within the module, and the parentheses ( ) represent the space to pass data to the subroutine from another procedure. In most cases, you will leave the parentheses empty.

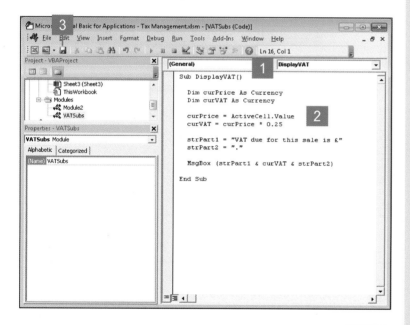

Create a subroutine

Create a subroutine

1 In a code module, type `Sub<name>( )`, where <name> is the name for your subroutine.

2 Between the `Sub` line and the `EndSub` line the Visual Basic Editor inserts for you, type the code you want to run.

3 Click the Save toolbar button or press Ctrl+S to save your work.

Important

If the Visual Basic Editor doesn't allow the name you use for your subroutine, you might have tried to use a reserved word, such as TIME or DATE. Try another name.

Important

The name of your subroutine must begin with a letter and must not contain any spaces.

Create a function

Create a function

1. In a code module, type `Function<name> (argument1, argument2...)` where `<name>` is the name of your function and the `argument1` (and subsequent) values are the names of variables to be used in the function.

2. Between the `Function` line and `EndFunction` line the Visual Basic Editor inserts for you, type the code that will perform the function's calculations.

3. Before the `EndFunction` line, assign the result of the function's calculation to the function's name.

For your information

In this function, steps 2 and 3 are combined into a single line of code.

Excel is a powerful data management and analysis tool. You summarise your data using formulas, finding sums, averages and so on. If you want to define a customised calculation, such as CalculateVAT, you can do so by defining a function using VBA. You just define the calculation, indicate what arguments (data inputs) it should accept and you're ready to go. You may then create a formula such as =CalculateVAT(A2), which finds the VAT due on the sales amount in cell A2.

In the task, the 'Function', keyword indicates you are creating a function that should return a value. The 'name' refers to the name of the function and the 'arguments' are values the function uses in its calculations. For example, a function to calculate a 25 per cent VAT charge would generate a result of £25 on a sale of £100.

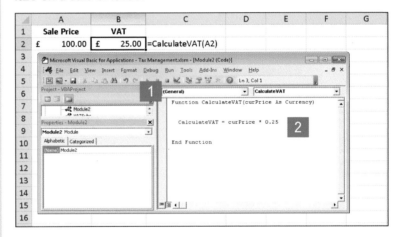

Jargon buster

An **argument** is a value used by a function. For example, the SUM function accepts one or more values, such as numbers or cell ranges, as arguments. If you create the workbook formula =SUM(A1:A2), then the cell range A1:A2 is the argument.

See also

For much more information on working with variables, see Chapter 3.

Even the simplest VBA routines can be a mystery to someone who encounters them for the first time. Equally, if you've used a workbook for a few years in your home-based business, you will feel the same if you can't remember what you had in mind. You can reduce that confusion by adding notes – called *comments* – to your code.

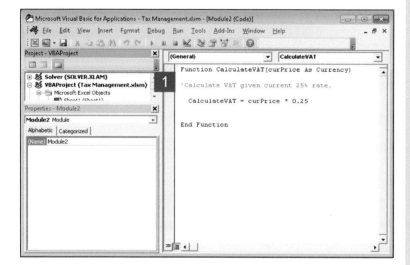

Add a comment to your code

1 Either:

   a. Type an apostrophe at the start of a line to make the entire line a comment.

   or:

   b. Add a comment to the right of a line of code by typing an apostrophe – everything to the right of the apostrophe will be considered a comment and ignored when you run the routine.

Did you know?

If you want to try your VBA code without running a specific line, add an apostrophe to the start of the line to make it a comment.

Did you know?

The Visual Basic Editor displays comments in green text so they stand out.

Run a VBA routine

After you create a VBA routine, it's time to test it out by running it. Running a VBA routine, as the name implies, causes Excel to implement the steps laid out in your code.

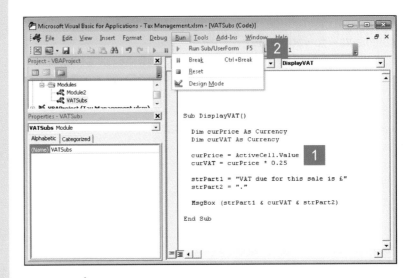

Run a VBA routine

1 Click in the VBA routine you want to run so the insertion point is within that block of code.

2 Either:

   a. Click the Run tab, then the Run Sub/UserForm menu item.

   or:

   b. Press F5.

See also

For more information on executing your code one line at a time, see Chapter 13.

When you create a code module in the Visual Basic Editor, the program assigns it a descriptive but uninspiring name, such as Module1 or Module2. It makes sense to group routines with similar objectives, such as calculating tax, into the same module, so you should consider changing that module's name to reflect the code it contains.

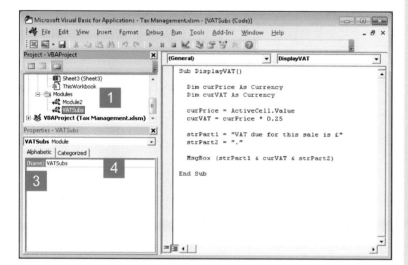

Rename a code module

1 In the Project panel, click the module you want to rename.

2 If necessary, press F4 to display the Properties Window.

3 Click the box next to the Name property.

4 Type a new name for the code module and press Enter.

Important

Your module name must start with a letter and not contain any spaces.

Delete a code module

As you work with VBA in Excel, you'll likely create some VBA routines that will, over time, become surplus to requirements. Just as deleting unneeded worksheets reduces clutter in your workbooks, so will deleting unneeded code modules reduce the clutter in your VBA projects.

Delete a code module

1 Display the Project window, then right-click the code module you want to delete.

2 Click the Remove Module menu item.

3 Decide whether or not to save the code module's contents to a text file:

a. If you want to export the code module to a text file, click Yes and follow the instructions to save the code in a file.

b. If you want to delete the code module without exporting its contents, click No.

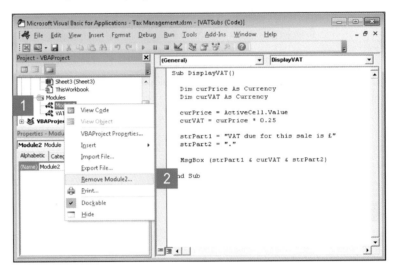

Important

Deleting a code module can't be reversed. Once you delete it, it's gone for good.

Did you know?

You can stop the deletion process by clicking the Cancel button in the dialog box that appears.

As you might have learned from hard experience, it is always wise to make backup copies of your files to prevent against possible loss. VBA code modules are no exception. You can export the contents of a code module to a text file and save it elsewhere to ensure you have a second copy in case your first is lost due to disk failure or accidental deletion.

◀ **Export a code module to a text file**

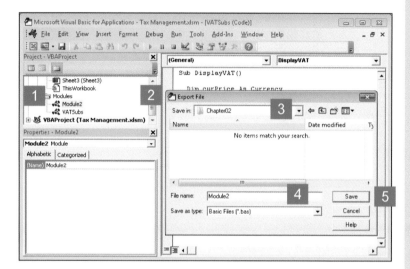

Export a code module to a text file

1 In the Project window, right-click the code module you want to export.

2 Click the Export File menu item.

3 Navigate to the folder where you want to store the file in the Save in box.

4 In the File name box, type a name for the file.

5 Click Save.

Important

Be sure to remember where you saved your file! Consider storing your exported code in the same folder as your workbook.

Did you know?

You can import a file into a VBA project by clicking the File tab, then the Import File menu item.

Working with data and variables

Introduction

After you create an Excel workbook, you populate it with data and formulas to summarise your data. In Excel VBA, you also use your worksheet data as fuel for your calculations, but you have much flexibility. Rather than just using the built-in functions to create worksheet formulas, you can develop procedures to perform custom calculations and other processes to meet your needs. Here, you will learn how to work with data and variables by declaring variables, arrays and the built-in Excel objects. The tasks are important background for the rest of the guide.

What you'll do

Understand data types in Excel VBA

Declare a variable

Require variable declaration before use

Manage variable scope

Perform calculations using mathematical operators

Define a constant

Define a static variable

Define an array

Define a multidimensional array

Redefine an array

Define a dynamic array

Display an object type

Define an object variable

Understand data types in Excel VBA

When you add data to an Excel worksheet, the program examines the data and assigns the most likely data formatting. Those formats include dates, times, numbers and 'general' for text or mixed entries. In Excel VBA, you assign each variable a data type. Table 3.1 lists the most common data types you will use in your calculations.

Table 3.1 Commonly used data types in Excel VBA

Data type	Description
Byte	Positive integer numbers from 0 to 255
Boolean	0 (False) or 1 (True)
Integer	Whole numbers from −32,768 to 32,767
Long	Whole numbers from −2,147,483,648 to 2,147,483,647
Currency	Numbers from −922,337,203,685,477.5808 to 922,337,203,685,477.5807 (note the maximum of four places to the right of the decimal point)
Single	Values in the range −3.402823E38 to −1.401298E−45 for negative values, 1.401298E−45 to 3.402823E38 for positive values
Double	Values in the range −1.79769313486232E308 to −4.94065645841247E−324 for negative values, 4.94065645841247E−324 to 1.79769313486232E308 for positive values
Date	Dates and times, which are stored as numbers within the Excel system
String	Character data – numbers are treated as text
Variant	A flexible data type that can contain numerical data, strings, dates or special values, such as Empty and Null

Did you know?

The Long, Currency, Date and String data types are the ones most commonly used for home and small business operations.

Did you know?

If you divide one number by another, be sure to assign the result to a data type with a decimal component such as Currency, Single or Double.

Variables are containers that store a value. Like worksheet cells, which you refer to using references such as A1 or B14, you can refer to the contents of a variable using its name. If you store price data in a variable named curPrice, for example, you can calculate a discount for a frequent customer using an expression such as **curExtendedPrice=curPrice*0.9**.

Variable declaration statements follow this pattern:

Dim variable As type

For example, you could declare a curExtendedPrice variable of Currency type in a routine to calculate a discounted price:

```
Sub CalculateExtendedPrice()
Dim curExtendedPrice As Currency
curExtendedPrice = ActiveCell.Value * 0.9
MsgBox ("Price with discount is £" &
curExtendedPrice)
End Sub
```

Declare a variable

Declare a variable

1. Type **Dim<variablename>** to start defining your variable.

2. Type a space, then type the keyword **As**.

3. Type another space, followed by the data type for the variable and press Enter.

3

Did you know?

When you type the name of a data type, the Visual Basic Editor displays a list of possible types based on the text you enter. You can select a value from the list and press Tab to accept it.

Did you know?

To define multiple variables on a line, type a statement such as **DimcurPriceasCurrency, curTaxasCurrency**. Be sure to have an **as<type>** statement for each variable you create.

Require variable declaration before use

Require variable declaration before use

1 Above the first **Sub** or **Function** declaration in a code module, type **Option Explicit** on its own line.

Unlike many more rigorous programming languages, VBA doesn't require you to declare a variable before you use it. As a result, one of the most common sources of errors when writing VBA code is to misspell a variable's name. It's good practice to declare a variable before you use it, but it's easy to forget or just be lazy. If you want to force yourself to declare your variables before using them, type the words **OptionExplict** on their own line above the first **Sub** or **Function** line in the module.

For example, you could require variable declaration in a subroutine that calculates a discounted price:

```
Option Explicit
Sub CalculateExtendedPrice()
  Dim curExtendedPrice As Currency
  curExtendedPrice = ActiveCell.Value *
  0.9
  MsgBox ("Price with discount is £" &
curExtendedPrice)
End Sub
```

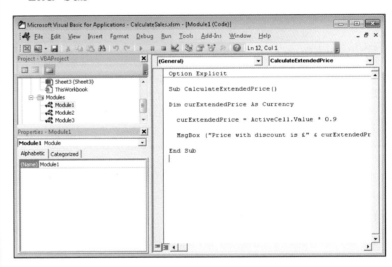

Important

The **Option Explicit** declaration only applies to the code module where you enter it.

Most Excel VBA routines are self-contained – there will usually be no reason to share variables between your routines. That said, there may be times when you want a variable to be available to every routine in a module or every module in that VBA project. These variables are referred to as global variables and, even though you might not use them frequently, they can come in handy when you need routines to share values.

You can define a global variable by writing the variable's **Dim** statement above the first **Sub** or **Function** line in a code module, as in the following sample:

```
Dim sngVATRate as Single
Sub CalculateVAT()
   Dim curVATDue As Currency
   sngVATRate = 0.25
   curVATDue = ActiveCell.Value *
   sngVATRate
End Sub
```

Manage variable scope

Manage variable scope

1 Click above the code for any functions or subroutines in a code module.

2 Define your global variable using a statement such as **DimsngVATRateas Single**.

3 If desired, add the keyword **Public** before the variable declaration so it will be available to every module in the VBA project.

3

!

Important

It's easy for a global variable to be updated unexpectedly in complex workbooks. If your variable contains a value you didn't expect, follow your code carefully to find the problem.

!

Important

You may not assign a value to a global variable in the declaration statement, just define it.

Perform calculations using mathematical operators

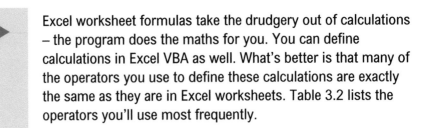

Excel worksheet formulas take the drudgery out of calculations – the program does the maths for you. You can define calculations in Excel VBA as well. What's better is that many of the operators you use to define these calculations are exactly the same as they are in Excel worksheets. Table 3.2 lists the operators you'll use most frequently.

Table 3.2 Arithmetic operators in Excel VBA

Data type	Description
+	Add two values
-	Subtract one value from another
^	Raise a value to an exponent (e.g. $2^3 = 8$)
*	Multiply two values
/	Divide one value by another
\	Divide one value by another and return the integer part of the result (e.g. 5\2 = 2)
Mod	Divide one value by another and return the remainder (e.g. 5 Mod 2 = 1)

Did you know?

You can also use parentheses to group operators into the desired order. For example, 8 * (2 + 4) produces a different result from 8 * 2 + 4.

Did you know?

The integer division and Mod operators are useful if you have a number of items in stock and want to know how many packs, perhaps of quantity 6, you could create from that stock.

You can create Excel VBA calculations to work out discounts, add purchases to find a grand total and so on. For values that don't change very often, such as discount rates for frequent purchasers or post and pack surcharges for a home-based business, you can define a constant and use it throughout your code module. If the value does change, you need only update a single line of code instead of searching for every occurrence within the module.

Constant definition statements follow this pattern:

```
Const variable = value
```

As an example, you could define a constant named sngVATRate and use it in a calculation:

```
Sub CalculateVAT()
   Dim curVATDue As Currency
   Const sngVATRate = 0.25
   curVATDue = ActiveCell.Value *
sngVATRate
End Sub
```

Define constant

Define a constant

1 In a code module, define a variable using the **Const** keyword and assign it a value.

2 One such statement might be **ConstsngVATRate=0.25**.

3

? Did you know?

If you define your constant above the first **Sub** or **Function** statement, any routine in the current module will be able to use the constant's value.

? Did you know?

If you add the keyword **Public** before the constant declaration (such as **PublicConstsngVATRate =0.25**), any module in the current project will be able to use the variable.

Define a static variable

One of the built-in features of Excel VBA is that the Visual Basic Editor resets every variable's value to zero when it runs a routine. The rationale for this action is that of ensuring data from previous operations doesn't affect the current one. That said, there might be times when you want a variable to hold its value until you close the VBA project. In that case, you can define a static variable.

Define a static variable

1 In a code module, define a variable using the **Static** keyword instead of the **Dim** keyword.

For example, you might want to calculate the total of every VAT calculation made while the workbook is open. You could do that by defining a static variable to hold the value:

```
Sub CalculateVAT()
    Static curVATDue As Currency
    Const sngVATRate = 0.25
    curVATDue = ActiveCell.Value *
sngVATRate
End Sub
```

?

Did you know?

If you define your static variable above the first **Sub** or **Function** statement, any routine in the current module can change its value.

When you manage a home-based business or track other items in Excel, you'll often find they come in sets. For example, you might have standard shipping rates for four regions – the UK, Europe, North America and the rest of the world. Rather than assign those values to four different variables, you can store them in an array. An *array* is like a box with several partitions – each compartment contains an item that is part of the set.

To define an array, you use a statement with the following structure:

```
Dim arrayname(items - 1) as type
```

For example, creating a four-element array to store shipping rates might use a command from this routine:

```
Sub SetShippingRates
Dim curShippingRates(3) As Currency
Dim i As Integer

For i = 0 To 3
  curShippingRates(i) = InputBox("Enter
a Shipping rate, please.")
Next

End Sub
```

Define an array

Define an array

1 Define an array using a statement such as **Dim curShippingRates(3) asCurrency**.

2 Fill the array from cell values or user input.

3

> **!**
>
> ### Important
>
> In Excel VBA, the first array element is number 0, so the array defined by the statement **Dim curShippingRates(3)** contains four elements.

Define a multidimensional array

Define a multidimensional array

1 Define an array using a statement such as `Dim curShippingRates (3,3)asCurrency`.

2 Fill the array from cell values or user input.

Just as you can define an array to hold a *single* series of values, such as shipping rates, you can define an array with *multiple* dimensions. For example, you could define a set of shipping rates by region and by speed of delivery. You could have separate rates for four regions – the UK, Europe, North America and the rest of the world. You might also have a dimension for delivery speed – surface mail, air mail, priority and overnight. Each rate would correspond to two values: region and delivery speed.

You're not limited to two-dimensional arrays. If you want to store multiple *types* of information, such as region, shipping rates, tax rates and customs fees, you could create an array with the required dimensions. In this case, you could create an array with four dimensions. The statement to define a multi-dimensional array follows this pattern:

```
Dim variable(dim1, dim2, …) as type
```

The following subroutine contains code that defines a two-dimensional array, with each dimension holding four values:

```
Sub SetShippingRates
Dim curShippingRates(3, 3) As Currency
Dim i As Integer
Dim j As Integer

For i = 0 To 3
  For j = 0 to 3
    curShippingRates(i) =
InputBox("Enter a shipping rate,
please.")
  Next
Next

End Sub
```

Circumstances change all of the time, even when you're writing VBA code. From time to time, you might find that you need to make an array larger or smaller while running a routine. For example, you might define an array with ten available colours for a product, then discover a particular model only has nine options. In that case, you can redefine an array so it is the proper size.

The statement to redefine an array is exactly the same as the statement to define it, except that you precede the line with `ReDim` instead of `Dim`. The following subroutine shows one case where you might use the `ReDim` statement:

```
Sub SetShippingRates
Dim curShippingRates(3) As Currency
Dim i As Integer
For i = 0 To 3
  curShippingRates(i) = InputBox("Enter
a shipping rate, please.")
Next
ReDim curShippingRates(4)
End Sub
```

Did you know?

You can keep Excel from deleting your existing array data by using the `Preserve` keyword in your `ReDim` statement (such as `ReDimPreserve curShippingRates(4)`).

Redefine an array

Redefine an array

1 Type a new definition for the array using the `ReDim` keyword, such as `ReDim curShippingRates(4)`.

3

Define a dynamic array

Define a dynamic array

1 Define the array using a statement without specifying the array size, such as **Dim curShippingRates ()**.

2 Use the **ReDim** statement to resize the array after you know how many items it should contain.

See also

For information on redefining an array, see earlier in this chapter.

Important

Remember that Excel VBA numbers array items from zero, so you should subtract one from the number of items to get the correct array size.

A *dynamic array* is an array without a specific size. Why would you create a dynamic array? One reason would be if you use Option Explicit to require variable declaration. If your array's size depends on user input or the size of a data set, defining a dynamic array puts it in place for you to work with later. After you know the size of the array, such as by gathering user input using an InputBox or by counting some group of items in the workbook, you can define the array's size using a **ReDim** statement.

The statement to declare a dynamic array follows this pattern:

```
Dim variable() as type
```

The following subroutine defines a dynamic array and then redefines it using the **ReDim** statement as soon as the user indicates how many values are to go into the array:

```
Sub SetShippingRates()

Dim curShippingRates() as Currency
Dim intItems As Integer
Dim i As Integer
intItems = InputBox("How many rates
will you enter?")
ReDim curShippingRates(intItems)
'Arrays count from 0, so subtract one
from rates to enter.
For I = 0 to intItems - 1
  curShippingRates(i) =
InputBox("Enter a shipping rate,
please.")
Next
End Sub
```

So far in this chapter you have encountered variables that refer to numbers, strings of characters and so on. You can also use variables to refer to Excel objects, such as workbooks, worksheets and cell ranges. Excel is a vast program with many components, so it would be impossible to remember every object available to you in VBA. You can explore these Excel objects, as well as the elements they contain, by using the Object Browser.

To display a type of object, click an item in the Classes panel. You can view the members of the class in the Members panel to the right of the Classes list and get more information on the members by double-clicking any item of interest.

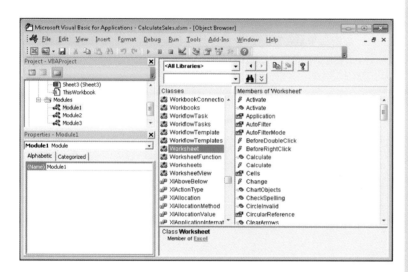

Did you know?

You can also display the Object Browser by pressing F2 within the Visual Basic Editor.

Display an object type

1 Click the View tab, then the Object Browser menu item.

2 Click the class you want to display.

3 Scroll through the available members of the class.

4 Click the Close button to close the Object Browser.

3

Define an object variable

Define an object variable

1 Define a variable as an object type, using a statement such as **DimwksAs Worksheet**.

2 Assign an object of that type to the variable, using a statement such as **Set wks=ThisWorkbook. Worksheets ("FebruaryTax")**.

3 Write code related to the object, using a statement such as **wks.Tab.Color =vbGreen**.

4 At the end of your subroutine, use a statement such as **Setwks=Nothing** to release the memory assigned to the object.

If you want to refer to an Excel object such as a workbook, worksheet or cell range, you can do so by defining an object variable. As the name implies, an *object variable* refers to an object. After you define an object variable and assign a specific item, such as a worksheet, to it, you can refer to that object using the variable name.

The following code sample assigns the worksheet named FebruaryTax to the **wks** object variable. The **wks** variable's name looks like the word *worksheet*, which is the object type to which it refers.

```
Sub SetMailingRates()
Dim wks As Worksheet
  Set wks = ThisWorkbook.Worksheets
("FebruaryTax")
  wks.Tab.Color = vbGreen
  Set wks = Nothing
End Sub
```

See also

For more information on referring to object variables and their components (such as a worksheet's name) using a minimum of code, see Chapter 12.

Managing workbooks and files

4

Introduction

All of your Microsoft Excel data is contained within one or more workbooks. Just like Word documents or PowerPoint presentations, you should divide your data between your workbooks so similar information is grouped together. For example, sales data could reside in one workbook and customer data in another. The more complicated your enterprise, the more likely it is that you will have multiple files. Here you'll find information on manipulating your workbooks by performing tasks such as opening workbooks, allowing users to select which workbook to open and closing and deleting workbooks.

Managing workbooks and files 57

Open a workbook

If you've worked with Excel for any length of time, it's likely that you have created several workbooks you open frequently. One common task might be to copy information between workbooks. If you want, you can create a VBA routine to automate that process. To do so successfully, both the source workbook and the target workbook must be open.

To open a workbook, you use the **Workbooks** object's **Open** method. The **Open** method has numerous arguments you can set, such as if the file has a password, to update links to external data sources, save the file using the local language setting and so on. The arguments you will use most frequently are:

Open a workbook

1. Create a subroutine.

2. In the body of the subroutine, enter a line of code that contains these elements:

   a. **Workbooks.Open** (followed by a space).

   b. The **FileName**, including the path to the file and the file's name.

   c. Whether to open the file in **ReadOnly** mode or not.

- **FileName**, which specifies the folder and name of the file. For example, the file's path might be **c:\Users\Curt\ Documents** and the file name **Sales.xlsx**, resulting in a **FileName** value of **c:\Users\Curt\Documents\ Sales.xlsx**.

- **ReadOnly**, which can be set to **True** or **False**. This argument specifies whether the workbook should open in read only mode or not.

An example of a well-formed VBA statement using the **Open** method would be:

```
Workbooks.Open Filename:="c:\Files\
Sales.xlsx", ReadOnly:=False
```

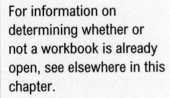

See also

For information on determining whether or not a workbook is already open, see elsewhere in this chapter.

Important

When you look through the **Open** method's help file, you'll see that it's possible to add a file's password to the **Open** method's argument list. You shouldn't do so. It's a poor security practice that could permit unauthorised users to open a restricted file.

Excel is a very flexible program. One of the ways that it makes your life easier is to let you open files that aren't stored in the native Excel format. For example, if a colleague sends you a text file that contains data from another program, you can often open that file in Excel. All you need to do is let Excel know how to deal with the text file before you open it.

To open a text file in Excel, you use the **Workbooks** object's **Open** method. In addition to specifying the file's path and name, you should indicate two other items: whether or not to open the file in read only mode and the file's delimiter. If your code opens the workbook in read only mode, you can view the new file's contents but not edit them.

A *delimiter* is a character used to separate one cell's value from the next. You can use any character as a delimiter, but the most common delimiter characters are punctuation marks and tabs as they are unlikely to occur in a data file.

■ **FileName** specifies the folder and name of the file. For example, the file's path might be **c:\Users\Curt\ Documents** and the filename **Sales.txt**, resulting in a **FileName** value of **c:\Users\Curt\Documents\ Sales.txt**.

■ **ReadOnly** can be set to **True** or **False**. This argument specifies whether the workbook should open in read only mode or not.

■ **Delimiter** identifies the character used to delimit the data set.

An example of a well-formed VBA statement that opens a text file with tab characters as the delimiter is:

```
Workbooks.Open Filename:="c:\Files\
Sales.txt", ReadOnly:=False, _
Delimiter:=Chr(9)
```

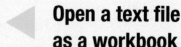

Open a text file as a workbook

Open a text file as a workbook

1 Create a subroutine.

2 Add a line of code that contains these elements:

a. **Workbooks.Open** (followed by a space).

b. The **Filename**, including the full path.

c. The **Delimiter**

?

Did you know?

The most common delimiter is the comma. You might see files with a .csv extension – those files are text files with comma-separated values, hence the extension.

4

i

For your information

The Chr(9) statement represents a tab. You can also enclose the delimiter character in quotes, such as ",", "/", or "|".

Open a file the user selects

▶

If you create a VBA routine that always uses the same file that's stored in the same directory, you can include the file's path and name in the **Open** method statement. However, if the exact file will change with time, you can create a VBA routine that lets you select a workbook using the Open dialog box.

Your VBA routine should consist of three elements: declaring a variable to hold the name of the file the user selects, a statement that displays the Open dialog box and assigns its output to the variable you created, plus a statement that calls the **Workbooks.Open** method to open the file.

Open a file the user selects

1 Create a subroutine.

2 In the body of the subroutine, do the following:

a. Define a variable to store the filename and path.

b. Assign the output of the **Open** dialog box to the variable.

c. Invoke the **Open** method to open the file the user identified.

The Open dialog box lets the user select which file to open and returns the file's full path and name, which is precisely the information the **Open** method's **FileName** argument requires.

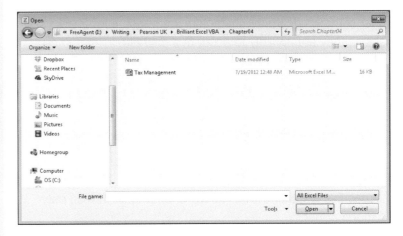

```
Dim varFileName as Variant
varFileName = Application.
GetOpenFilename
Workbooks.Open Filename:=varFileName
```

There are few things more frustrating than doing good work on a spreadsheet and then losing it because you forgot to save what you did. You should save your workbook every time you make an important change, which you could define as something you would hate to have to do again. If your routines make significant changes to your workbooks, you should consider creating VBA code that saves those changes as you go.

The **Workbook** object's **Save** method requires a reference to a workbook, followed by a full stop, followed by the word **Save**, with no spaces. For example, you could create any of the following lines of code:

```
ActiveWorkbook.Save
Workbooks("Sales.xlsx").Save
Workbooks(1).Save
```

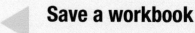

Save a workbook

Save a workbook

1 Create a subroutine.

2 In the body of the subroutine, type code that follows the pattern **reference.Save**, where **reference** identifies a workbook.

Important

It might take a moment for your computer's hard disk to spin up, so don't worry if Excel seems to hesitate for a brief moment.

4

Save a workbook in a different format

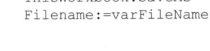

The Excel desktop program has two different ways to save a file: `Save` and `SaveAs`. Saving a file saves it under the same name, in the same folder, in the same format. You can change any of those elements by using the SaveAs method instead. Just as you can use `SaveAs` in the main Excel program, you can use VBA to display the built-in Save As dialog box. You can use that dialog box's controls to change the workbook's name, folder or format.

The `Workbook` object's `SaveAs` method requires a file name and path, which you can get by displaying the `SaveAs` dialog box. The following code is one way to do it:

Save a workbook in a different format

1 Create a subroutine.

2 In the body of the subroutine, type the following lines of code:

a. Define a variable to store the filename and path.

b. Assign the output of the Save As dialog box to the variable.

c. Invoke the `SaveAs` method to save the file the user identified in the folder and format identified using the Save As dialog box.

```
Dim varFileName
varFileName = Application.
GetSaveAsFilename
ThisWorkbook.SaveAs
Filename:=varFileName
```

See also

For more information on using built-in dialog boxes, see Chapter 11.

Important

The most common error in the `ThisWorkbook.SaveAs` statement is to forget to type a colon before the equal sign in `Filename:=varFileName`.

Many of your VBA routines will interact with other workbooks. For example, you might want to cut and paste data between files on your computer. For those procedures to work properly, you must ensure that the files are open. However, if you try to open a workbook that is already open, the routine might result in an error. To avoid the possibility of that occurrence, you should check if the file you want to work with is already open.

The following code sample is significantly longer than the others in this chapter, but that's because it has more work to do. The routine's goal is to check every open workbook to determine whether or not that workbook's name matches the name of the workbook you want to open. If the workbook is already open, then you can exit the subroutine without trying to open the already open file.

After the subroutine declaration, the code identifies three variables: the first is used to refer to workbooks, the second to indicate whether the workbook is open or not and the third to store the filename. After that, it sets the **bOpen** value to **False** and then assigns a value to the string **strFileName** variable. The code won't actually work as written, because there is no filename – the text **<filename>** is simply a placeholder. You would need to get the target filename from the user, either by having them type in the name directly or by selecting the name using the Open dialog box.

The next section of the code uses a **For...Each** loop to examine every workbook that is currently open in Excel. If the name of the workbook matches the **strFileName** variable's value, then the routine displays a message box indicating the workbook is already open and exits the subroutine. If none of the filenames matches, the routine displays a message indicating the workbook is not open.

Detect if a workbook is open

Detect if a workbook is open

1. Create a subroutine.

2. In the body of the subroutine, type the code sample from the next page.

3. Replace **<filename>** with the name of the file, including directory path and extension, that you want to open.

4

See also

For more information on using object variables, see Chapter 3.

Detect if a workbook is open (cont.)

See also

For more information on using **For**...**Next** loops, see Chapter 12.

When you use this code in your own workbooks, it is unlikely that you would display a message box indicating if a workbook is open. Instead, if the workbook you want to use is open, you can go ahead and use the code in the rest of the routine to cut and copy your data or perform some other task. If the desired workbook is *not* open, then you could use VBA code to open it before continuing on with the task at hand.

Here is the code sample:

```
Sub CheckIfOpen()
Dim w as Workbook
Dim bOpen as Boolean
Dim strFileName as String

bOpen = False
strFileName = "<filename>"
For Each w in Application.Workbooks
If w.Name = strFileName Then
 bOpen = True
 MsgBox "The named workbook is open."
 Exit Sub
End If
Next
If bOpen = False Then
 MsgBox "The named workbook is not
open."
End If
End Sub
```

Modern computers have bags of storage and memory, but it is still a good habit to close any workbooks you aren't working with at the moment. Doing so frees up program resources and makes it easier to locate a specific file you want to work with. Closing a workbook is straightforward, but you should always be sure to offer the option of saving your work before doing so.

To use the **Workbook** object's **Close** method, you need to identify the workbook you want close, type a full stop, then type **Close**. There are many ways to refer to workbooks in Excel VBA – the lines of code below show just a few of those options:

```
ThisWorkbook.Close
ActiveWorkbook.Close
Workbooks("<filename>").Close
ThisWorkbook.Close SaveChanges:=True
```

The final example also introduces the **SaveChanges** argument. If you set the **SaveChanges** argument to **True**, then Excel saves all of your work before closing the workbook. If you set the **SaveChanges** argument to **False**, then Excel closes the workbook and discards any changes you made since last time you saved the file.

Close a workbook

Close a workbook

1 Create a subroutine.

2 Enter one of the following lines of code:

a. **ThisWorkbook.Close**

b. **ActiveWorkbook. Close**

c. **Workbooks ("<filename>"). Close**

d. **ThisWorkbook.Close SaveChanges:=True**

4

Did you know?

You can add the **SaveChanges** argument to any of the lines of code shown above.

Did you know?

If you have unsaved changes in a workbook you want to close, Excel will prompt you to save them.

Create a new workbook

As you continue to work in Excel VBA, you will most likely find the need to create new workbooks. For example, if you do monthly reporting for your home-based business or send updates to your accountant, then you might create monthly summaries of your business activities. You can always keep those records in a single workbook, but you might find it easiest to parcel out your information by month or year, with each *new* month or year in its own workbook.

Creating a new workbook in Excel VBA is extremely straightforward. The command to do so is:

```
Workbooks.Add
```

You can use an existing workbook as a template for the **Workbooks.Add** method. The code would look like this:

```
Workbooks.Add("c:\path\filename")
```

where **c:\path\filename** is the path and full name (including its extension, such as .xlsx) of the workbook to be used as the template.

Create a new workbook

1. Create a subroutine.

2. Enter the following line of code in the body of the subroutine:

```
Workbooks.Add
```

For your information

Some corporate IT environments prohibit users from creating files using VBA code. If you have trouble using the **Add** method, check with your IT department to see if such a restriction is in place.

There will be times when a file on your computer is surplus to requirements. The data might be old or perhaps you have redesigned your workbook and copied your data to a new file. If that's the case, then you can use Excel VBA to delete the workbook when it's no longer needed. Deleting a file is sometimes necessary, but should not be undertaken lightly.

To delete an Excel workbook, you need to identify the file by assigning its name to a variable and then using the Kill command to delete it. The most common way to select a file to delete is to use a dialog box such as the Open dialog box or the Save As dialog box. The following code example uses the Save As dialog box to identify the file to be deleted:

```
Dim strName As String
strName = Application.
GetSaveAsFilename(Title:="File to
Delete")
Kill (strName)
```

Did you know?

If you want to delete every file with a specific extension, such as .txt for text files, you can use the filename `"*.txt"`. The * tells Excel to delete every file with the named extension. Be careful, though!

Delete a file

1 Create a subroutine.

2 Enter the following lines of code in the body of the subroutine:

  a. **DimstrNameAs String**

  b. **strName = Application.Get SaveAsFilename (Title:="File to Delete")**

  c. **Kill(strName)**

Important

You can't delete an open workbook.

4

Managing worksheets

Introduction

Excel worksheets can contain data of many different types. In most cases, each worksheet within a workbook will contain a specific subset of the overall data you store within the workbook. When you create programs using Excel VBA, you will often find reasons to create, manipulate – even delete – worksheets within your workbooks. The actual commands for making these changes are reasonably straightforward, but there are some subtleties that you will need to keep in mind. So long as you ensure that your worksheet-related commands reflect the state of your workbook when they are executed, you should have no problems.

What you'll do

Add a worksheet

Delete a worksheet

Move a worksheet

Copy a worksheet

Hide or unhide a worksheet

Rename a worksheet

Protect a worksheet

Print a worksheet

Add a worksheet

Every Excel workbook must contain at least *one* worksheet, but most workbooks will contain multiple worksheets. For example, if you store a year's worth of data in a single workbook, you should consider creating a worksheet for each month. Doing so divides your data into manageable units and lets you find the specific data you're looking for more easily.

To add a sheet to a workbook, you use the `Sheet` collection's `Add` method. For example, if you wanted to add a worksheet to the same workbook that contains your VBA code, you could use the code snippet `ThisWorkbook.Sheets.Add`. You can also use several other parameters to identify the position of the sheet you add, the number of sheets to be added and type of sheet to be added.

Add a worksheet

1. Create a subroutine.

2. In the body of the subroutine, type `ThisWorkbook.Sheets.Add`

3. If desired, use any of the following parameters to specify where and what type of sheets to add:
   a. `Before`
   b. `After`
   c. `Count`
   d. `Type`

■ `Before` identifies the existing sheet before which you place the new sheets. If you leave this parameter out, Excel adds the sheet before the active sheet.

■ `After` identifies the existing sheet after which you place the new sheets.

■ `Count` indicates the number of sheets to be added.

■ `Type` identifies the type of sheet to be added to your workbook. You can select from the sheet types `xlWorksheet`, `xlChart`, `xlExcel4MacroSheet` and `xlExcel4IntlMacroSheet`. If you leave this parameter blank, the `Add` method inserts a worksheet.

As an example, you could use the following code to add two worksheets after the sheet named Sheet2:

```
ThisWorkbook.Sheets.Add
After:=Worksheets("Sheet2"), Count:=2
```

This variation of the code would add a chart sheet at the beginning of the workbook:

```
ThisWorkbook.Sheets.Add
Before:=Worksheets(1), Type:=xlChart
```

Important

You may use either the `Before` or `After` argument, but not both.

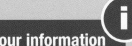

For your information

You *can* add any number of worksheets to your workbook, but it's best not to add more than you need.

Excel workbooks are similar to many other projects in the sense that you are never truly done changing them. Whether you add new data, change the formulas on a worksheet or modify worksheet formatting, you will probably find new ways to work more effectively. If you find that your changes make one of your worksheets redundant, you can delete that sheet.

The VBA command to delete a worksheet relies on the `Sheets` collection's `Delete` method. All you need to do is identify the sheet you want to get rid of, either by the number of the sheet within the workbook or by entering the sheet's name. The following two code snippets provide an example of each approach:

```
Sheets(1).Delete
Sheets("Sheet1").Delete
```

When you attempt to delete a worksheet that contains data, whether by using the user interface or VBA, Excel displays a confirmation dialog box asking if you're sure you want to delete the worksheet. You can temporarily disable alert boxes by adding the command `Application.DisplayAlerts = False` on a line before you invoke the Delete method.

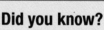

For your information

Be sure to set the `DisplayAlerts` property to `True` after you delete the worksheet. Not doing so could cause you to miss other important warnings.

Delete a worksheet

1 Create a subroutine.

2 In the body of the subroutine, use one of the following code patterns:

  a. `Sheets(1).Delete`

  b. `Sheets ("sheetname"). Delete`

Did you know?

You can also use an InputBox (see Chapter 11) to enter the name of the worksheet to be deleted.

5

Move a worksheet

Move a worksheet

1 Create a subroutine.

2 In the body of the subroutine, use one of the following code patterns:

a. `Sheets(1).Move` – which moves the numbered worksheet to a *new* workbook.

b. `Sheets(2).Move, Before:=Sheets(1)` – moves the numbered worksheet *before* the first worksheet.

c. `Sheets(1).Move, After:=Sheets(3)` – moves the numbered worksheet *after* the third worksheet.

You will often find that the data contained in one workbook could be useful in another. If that's the case, you can move a worksheet to another workbook or, if you find your workflow isn't as efficient as it might be, you can relocate a worksheet within the same workbook. Moving a worksheet doesn't leave a copy of the worksheet in its original position – as the name implies, it cuts the worksheet from its original position and pastes it in its new position.

You can move a worksheet quickly using Excel VBA by using the `Sheets` collection's `Move` method. Using the `Move` method by itself, without indicating a destination for the sheet you're moving, causes Excel VBA to move the sheet to a new workbook. If you want to move the worksheet within the current workbook, you can use one of the `Move` method's two optional parameters: `Before` and `After`.

■ `Before` identifies the existing sheet before which you place the moved sheets. If you leave this parameter out, Excel moves the sheet to before the active sheet.

■ `After` identifies the existing sheet after which you place the moved sheets.

For your information

If you try to move a worksheet after a worksheet that doesn't exist – such as Sheet(4) in a workbook with three worksheets – the `Move` method will generate an error.

Did you know?

You can also use worksheet names, enclosed in double quotes, instead of sheet numbers in these commands. For example, `Sheets("January").Move`.

Just as you can move a worksheet to another workbook or within the same workbook, you can create a *copy* of a worksheet and move it. For example, you could use a worksheet as a template and copy it within your existing workbook. You can also use copying to include a data set in another workbook without deleting the original worksheet.

If you use the `Copy` method by itself without indicating a target destination for the sheet you're copying, Excel VBA copies the sheet to a new workbook. If you want to copy the worksheet within the current workbook, you can use one of the `Copy` method's two optional parameters – `Before` and `After`.

- `Before` identifies the existing sheet before which you place the copied sheet. If you leave this parameter out, Excel copies the sheet and places it before the active sheet.

- `After` identifies the existing sheet, after which Excel will place the copied sheet.

Did you know?

As with moving worksheets, you can also use worksheet names, enclosed in double quotes, instead of sheet numbers in these commands. For example, `Sheets("January").Copy`.

For your information

Trying to copy a worksheet to a position before or after a worksheet that doesn't exist will result in an error. Be sure you create error-handling code to manage these situations (see Chapter 13).

Copy a worksheet

Copy a worksheet

1 Create a subroutine.

2 In the body of the subroutine, use one of the following code patterns:

  a. `Sheets(1).Copy`
    – copies the numbered worksheet to a new workbook.

  b. `Sheets(2).Copy, Before:=Sheets(1)`
    – copies the numbered worksheet to before the first worksheet.

  c. `Sheets(1).Copy, After:=Sheets(3)`
    – copies the numbered worksheet to after the third worksheet.

5

Hide or unhide a worksheet

Hide or unhide a worksheet

1 Create a subroutine.

2 In the body of the subroutine, type one of the following lines of code. The first example hides the worksheet, the second unhides it:

a. **Sheets(1).Visible = False**

b. **Sheets(1).Vislble = True**

Even if you work in a home-based business, your workbooks might contain data that you don't want to display to anyone who might use your computer. You can keep your data away from casual observers by hiding a worksheet. *Hiding* a worksheet doesn't delete it, so you can still use its contents in your formulas, but it does make if a little bit more difficult to find the data unless you know what you're looking for.

The **Visible** property indicates whether a worksheet appears in the body of the workbook or not. You can both read the **Visible** property to discover if a worksheet is visible or hidden and change the property's value to control whether or not the worksheet appears on the tab bar. The following two code snippets are valid uses of the **Visible** property. The first hides Sheets(1) and the second displays the sheet named Sheet3.

```
Sheets(1).Visible = False
Sheets("Sheet3").Visible = True
```

Did you know?

Users can still unhide a worksheet by clicking the View tab, then unhide on the ribbon and selecting a hidden sheet from the dialog box that appears.

When you create an Excel 2010 workbook, it contains three sheets named Sheet1, Sheet2 and Sheet3. These names aren't very descriptive, so the program lets you rename your worksheets. If you rename a worksheet as part of an automated process, you might use the month the data represents, the name of a product or the name of a customer. Doing so makes it easier to recognise each worksheet's contents when you look through the workbook.

You can encode the new name for a worksheet in your VBA routine, but it's more likely that you'll want the flexibility to name the new worksheet by typing in a value. To allow you and your colleagues to do that, display an InputBox and use the control's output for the sheet's new name. One such code snippet might be:

```
Dim strName
strName = InputBox("New name for the
sheet?")
ActiveSheet.Name = strName
```

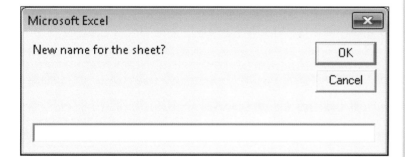

Rename a worksheet

Rename a worksheet
1. Create a subroutine.
2. In the body of the subroutine, type the following code:
   a. `Dim strName`
   b. `strName = InputBox("New name for the sheet?")`
   c. `ActiveSheet.Name = strName`

!

Important

You cannot have two worksheets with the same name within a workbook.

See also

For more information on using InputBoxes, see Chapter 11.

5

Protect a worksheet

Protect a worksheet

1 Create a subroutine.

2 Either:

  a. Enter a line of code such as `Worksheets(1).Protect`

  or:

  b. Use an InputBox to get a password and assign it using the `Password` parameter.

As mentioned earlier in this chapter, hiding a worksheet doesn't prevent users from displaying and changing that worksheet if they know what to do. If you want to require a password to change a worksheet in this way, you can do so by protecting the worksheet in this way. As the name implies, protecting a worksheet is much more secure than not doing so and will keep your data safe from casual alteration.

The **Protect** method has many different parameters you can set, but the most useful one is the **Password** parameter. Setting the **Password** parameter requires users to enter the pass phrase you define before they can delete the worksheet or alter its contents. The following code samples show two ways to protect a sheet. The first snippet doesn't set a password, the second one does.

```
Worksheets(1).Protect

Dim strPassword As String
strPassword = InputBox("Enter a password
for this sheet.")
ActiveSheet.Protect
Password:=strPassword
```

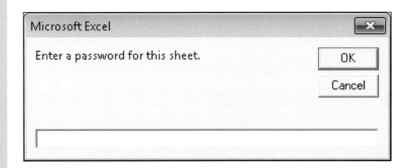

Important

Don't forget your password! Excel 2010 uses strong encryption, so it's highly unlikely you would be able to recover it.

Important

Protecting a worksheet without assigning a password allows anyone to turn off protection by clicking the Review tab, then Unprotect Sheet on the ribbon.

Businesses and organisations of all sizes conduct increasing amounts of business electronically. Even so, it still helps to print out a copy of an Excel worksheet every now and then. In Excel VBA, all you need to do is identify the worksheet you want to print out and whether or not you want to display a preview of what will be printed. Displaying a preview gives you the opportunity to cancel the print job if the command results don't reflect what you want.

By default, the `PrintOut` method prints one copy of the entire named worksheet. If you want print an area of the page, such as the cell range A1:G4, you need to define a print area. To do that, you use the `PageSetup` object's `PrintArea` method. One such command would be:

```
ActiveSheet.PageSetup.PrintArea=
"$A$1:$G$4".
```

The `PrintOut` method has many useful parameters that mimic the controls you'll find on the Print page of Backstage view. They are:

- **From** indicates the number of the page from which to start printing – if omitted, Excel prints starting with the first page.

- **To** gives the page to be printed – if omitted, Excel prints to the end of the worksheet

- **Copies** indicates the number of copies to print – if left blank, one copy is printed

- **Preview** controls whether to display a preview or not. The **Preview** parameter may be either **True** or **False** and, if omitted, is assumed to be false

- **ActivePrinter** lets you define the active printer on your system

- **PrintToFile** can be **True** or **False** – this parameter indicates whether the worksheet should be printed to a file or to the active printer and, if to a file, you must provide a ~~·~~ for the **PrToFileName** parameter

Print a worksheet

Print a worksheet

1 Create a subroutine.

2 Enter a line of code that identifies the sheet to be printed and any parameters to use.

5

- **Collate** can be **True** or **False**, telling Excel whether or not to collate multiple copies of the print job

- **PrToFileName** is required if the **PrintToFile** parameter is **True**, for the file to which the sheet should be printed

- **IgnorePrintAreas** directs Excel to print the entire worksheet even if the file has print areas defined for that sheet.

The following code snippets are valid uses of the **PrintOut** method. The first prints the first worksheet in the workbook, while the second displays a preview.

```
Worksheets(1).PrintOut
```

Did you know?

To clear a print area, use the command
ActiveSheet.PageSetup.PrintArea = False.

```
Worksheets(1).PrintOut, Preview:=True
```

Managing ranges

Introduction

In the previous two chapters, you learned how to work with the larger-scale building blocks of Excel files. First, you learned how to manipulate workbooks, which are the container for your Excel data. After that, you learned how to manipulate worksheets, which are the organisational units within a workbook. This chapter and the next describe how to work with the final level of Excel workbook organisation – individual cells and cell ranges. In this chapter, you will learn how to activate and select cell ranges, refer to other cells, insert and delete cell ranges, work with named ranges and resize rows and columns so they present your data in its best light.

What you'll do

Activate a cell range

Select a cell range

Select the active region

Refer to cells using `Offset`

Insert a cell range

Delete a cell range

Hide worksheet columns or rows

Create a named range

Resize a selected range

Set the column width

Set the row height

Activate a cell range

There are two ways to interact with groups of cells in your worksheet: activating the cells and selecting them. The technical distinctions are a bit subtle, but the main difference is that the **Activate** method only operates on a single group of cells, while the **Select** method lets you work with multiple groups of cells.

One other reason to use the **Activate** method as opposed to the **Select** method is speed of processing. Selecting a cell takes a lot longer than activating a cell does, so any complicated or long-running routines you create should use the **Activate** method whenever possible. The difference in speed is not that noticeable when there are only one or two actions in your code, but any routine that could make dozens or hundreds of individual selections will run noticeably slower than similar code using **Activate**.

The following code snippet shows how to activate cell A13:

```
Range("A13").Activate
```

Activate a cell range

1 Create a subroutine.

2 In the body of the subroutine, use the following code pattern:

```
Range.("cell_range").Activate
```

See also

For more information on using the **Offset** property, see Refer to cells using **Offset**, later in this chapter.

Did you know?

If a cell range is highlighted in your worksheet, the **ActiveCell** is the cell you first clicked when you highlighted the cells.

Selecting a cell range lets you perform operations such as cutting or copying cells. You select a range by identifying the cells you want to select and calling the `Select` method. The example code in the task demonstrates that there are several ways to identify ranges, including non-contiguous ranges.

If you want to select a non-contiguous range of cells, you separate the individual cell ranges using a comma. For example, if you wanted to select cells in the range B4:C6 and in the range F4:G6, you would write the command as `Range("B4:C6, F4:G6").Select`.

	A	B	C	D	E	F	G
1							
2		Month					
3	Day	January	February	March	April	May	June
4	1	43	180	38	175	61	54
5	2	29	129	199	178	113	103
6	3	22	24	54	106	88	155
7	4	170	46	38	124	142	106
8	5	49	166	26	36	34	52
9	6	34	194	99	171	137	48
10	7	93	130	195	81	47	65

Did you know?

Selecting a cell range is slower than activating a cell range. If you can use the `Activate` method instead of the `Select` method, your code will run faster.

Did you know?

You are not limited to selecting two ranges of cells when you use the select method. Commands such as `Range("A1:B3, A6:B9, A9:B12").Select` work just as well.

Select a cell range

6

Select a cell range

1 Create a subroutine.

2 In the body of the subroutine, use one of the following code patterns:

a. `Range("cell").Select`

b. `Range("range").Select`

c. `Range("range1, range2...").Select`

Select the active region

One of the most useful selection procedures in Excel 2010 is also one of the least well known. Suppose you have a block of 40 or 50 cells and you want to select all of them. Rather than identify the entire cell range, such as A2:G10, you can click any cell in the range and then select the *active region*, which is also called the *current region*. The active region doesn't extend beyond a blank row or column, but single cells at the edge of the region can affect how Excel identifies the region.

Selecting the active region is exactly what Excel does when you create an Excel table from a data list or filter or sort worksheet data. If you use the **ActiveCell.CurrentRegion.Select** method to select worksheet cells, it will identify a rectangular area with limits defined by the first blank row, column or worksheet edge that it encounters in each direction.

Select the active region

1. Create a subroutine.

2. In the body of the subroutine, use the following code:

```
ActiveCell.
CurrentRegion.
Select
```

	A	B	C	D	E	F	G	H
1								
2		Month						
3	Day	January	February	March	April	May	June	
4	1	43	180	38	175	61	54	
5	2	29	129	199	178	113	103	
6	3	22	24	54	106	88	155	
7	4	170	46	38	124	142	106	
8	5	49	166	26	36	34	52	
9	6	34	194	99	171	137	48	
10	7	93	130	195	81	47	65	
11								

?

Did you know?

In an Excel worksheet, you can select the current region by pressing Ctrl+*.

For your information

Be sure to test your VBA code when you select the active region – you might be surprised at which cells it includes.

When you create a formula in an Excel worksheet, you can use either absolute or relative references. Absolute references do not change when you copy the formula to another cell. Relative references, however, do change. If you refer to cells in Excel VBA using the offset property, you tell the program to affect a cell in a position relative to the active cell.

The `Offset` property accepts two arguments:

- **`Rows`** indicates the number of rows to move above or below the active cell – positive numbers tell Excel to move down, while negative numbers have Excel move above the active cell.

- **`Columns`** indicates the number of columns to move to the left or right of the active cell – positive numbers tell Excel to move to the right, while negative numbers have Excel move to the left.

It is the combination of the row and column values that identifies the new cell your VBA code will affect. For example, `ActiveCell.Offset(1, 2).Select` would select the cell one row below and two columns to the right of the active cell. If the active cell were B4, the cell referred to would be C6.

◢	A	B	C	D	E	F	G
1							
2		Month					
3	Day	January	February	March	April	May	June
4	1	43	180	38	175	61	54
5	2	29	129	199	178	113	103
6	3	22	24	54	106	88	155
7	4	170	46	38	124	142	106
8	5	49	166	26	36	34	52
9	6	34	194	99	171	137	48
10	7	93	130	195	81	47	65
11							

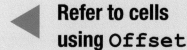

Refer to cells using `Offset`

6

Refer to cells using `offset`

1 Create a subroutine.

2 In the body of the subroutine, use the following code pattern:

```
ActiveCell.
Offset(rows,
columns).Attribute
```

?

Did you know?

If you refer to a cell that isn't on the worksheet (such as a cell two rows above cell A1), the Visual Basic Editor displays an error message.

Insert a cell range

Insert a cell range

1. Create a subroutine.

2. Enter code that uses the following pattern in the body of the subroutine:

```
Range(reference).
Insert Shift :=
direction
```

From time to time, you might want to insert a cell range into another group of cells. For example, suppose you forgot to enter a row of data into a list. Rather than cut and paste data from the list to make a blank row, you can insert a group of cells to make room for the new data.

You insert a range of cells using the **Range** object's **Insert** method. The **Insert** method has the syntax **Range(reference).Insert (direction)**. The **reference** argument denotes a range of cells, which could be a single cell or group of cells. The first cell in the reference should be at the top left corner of the range were you want to insert the new cells. For example, if you forgot to enter data into cells D3 to F5, you would use the command **Range(D3:F5).Insert**.

When you insert the cells, you can also specify an **XlShiftDirection** parameter to have Excel shift the cells down (**xlShiftDown**) or to the right (**xlShiftToRight**). If you don't specify a shift direction, Excel shifts the affected cells down.

As an example, suppose you have a worksheet with data in the range A2:G10. Using the command **Range("B10:G10").Insert Shift:=xlShiftDown** would insert cells in the range B10:G10, pushing the values in the existing cells down one row.

	A	B	C	D	E	F	G	H
1								
2		Month						
3	Day	January	February	March	April	May	June	
4	1	43	180	38	175	61	54	
5	2	29	129	199	178	113	103	
6	3	22	24	54	106	88	155	
7	4	170	46	38	124	142	106	
8	5	49	166	26	36	34	52	
9	6	34	194	99	171	137	48	
10	7							
11		93	130	195	81	47	65	
12								

Worksheet data changes frequently. On occasion, you will also have cause to change your worksheet structure by deleting cell ranges from your worksheet. You can delete cell ranges in Excel VBA by identifying the range and using the proper command. That command is the **Range** object's **Delete** method.

The **Delete** method uses two elements: the range of cells you want to delete and the direction the remaining cells should move once the cells are deleted. For example, you could delete cells in the range D4:F5 using the command **Range("D4:F5").Delete**.

You can also tell Excel in which direction to shift the remaining cells – either to the left (**xlShiftToLeft**) or up (**xlShiftUp**). In that case, the syntax of the command looks like this:

```
Range("D4:F5").Delete(xlShiftUp)
```

If you leave the **Shift** parameter blank, Excel shifts the remaining cells up.

	A	B	C	D	E	F	G	H
1								
2		Month						
3	Day	January	February	March	April	May	June	
4	1	43	180	38	175	61	54	
5	2	29	129	199	178	113	103	
6	3	22	24	54	106	88	155	
7	4	170	46	38	124	142	106	
8	5	49	166	26	36	34	52	
9	6	34	194				48	
10	7	93	130				65	
11								

Did you know?

If you delete cells using the **Range** object's **Delete** method, the data in those cells will be lost.

Delete a cell range

1 Create a subroutine.

2 Enter code that uses the following pattern in the body of the subroutine:

```
Range(reference).
Delete(direction)
```

For your information

Protecting a worksheet prevents you from adding or deleting cells.

Hide worksheet columns or rows

Worksheet columns and rows often contain a single type of data. Columns, for example, could contain information about a product's price. A row in the same worksheet might contain a full set of information about a product, such as its name, price and description. If you want to hide a row or column, you can do so using the code below. Bear in mind that you must refer to a column using its number, not letter designation (So column C is column 3).

You can hide a column or row using its **Hidden** property. Setting the property to **True** hides the column or row, while setting it to **False** displays it. The following examples of code snippets hide various columns and rows in a worksheet:

```
ActiveSheet.Columns(1).Hidden = True
ActiveSheet.Rows(3).Hidden = True
Sheets(1).Columns(3).Hidden = False
Sheets(2).Rows(8).Hidden = False
```

Hide worksheet columns or rows

1. Create a subroutine.

2. Enter code that uses one of the following patterns in the body of the subroutine:

   a. `ActiveSheet. Columns(number). Hidden = True`

   b. `ActiveSheet. Rows(number). Hidden = True`

   c. `ActiveSheet. Columns(number). Hidden = False`

   d. `ActiveSheet. Rows(number). Hidden = False`

   e. `ActiveSheet. Columns.Hidden = False  'Unhides all columns`

   f. `ActiveSheet.Rows. Hidden = False  'Unhides all rows`

	A	B	C	E	F	G
1						
2		Month				
3	Day	January	February	April	May	June
4	1	43	180	175	61	54
5	2	29	129	178	113	103
6	3	22	24	106	88	155
7	4	170	46	124	142	106
8	5	49	166	36	34	52
9	6	34	194	171	137	48
10	7	93	130	81	47	65
11						

Did you know?

A useful mnemonic for determining the number of a column is to use the initialis EJOTY. Each letter in that list is five positions after the previous one, so the E is at position 5, J at position 10, O at position 15, T at position 20 and Y at position 25.

If you want to hide or unhide every column or row, use the `Columns` or `Rows` object without specifying a column or row to hide or unhide. For example, the first snippet below unhides all columns, while the second unhides all rows:

```
ActiveSheet.Columns.Hidden = False
ActiveSheet.Rows.Hidden = False
```

Hiding column D using the command **ActiveSheet.Columns(4).Hidden = True** produces the result shown in the screenshot.

Did you know?

You can always unhide a column or row from the user interface by selecting the rows or columns on either side of the hidden elements and clicking the View tab, then Unhide on the ribbon.

Did you know?

You can use the values in hidden rows or columns in your worksheet formulas and VBA code.

Create a named range

If you frequently use a specific cell range in your formulas, you can define that range as a named range. As the name implies, a named range is a cell range that you refer to using a label instead of the cell addresses at the top left and bottom right of the range. For example, if you had January sales in cells A2:A32, you could refer to that range using the name JanuarySales.

To create a named range using Excel VBA, you use the **Range** object's **Name** property. The syntax for the command is **Range (reference).Name = "range name"**. The reference can be any set of cells, but there are a few restrictions on how you can name ranges in Excel. First, the name may not contain any spaces and must begin with a letter. Second, the name of the range may not duplicate a reserved word, such as the name of a column, the name of a variable type, such as Currency, or names of existing Excel objects.

The following bit of sample code demonstrates how to create a named range called January Sales:

```
Range("B4:B10").Name = "JanuarySales"
```

Create a named range

1 Create a subroutine.

2 Enter code that uses the following pattern in the body of the subroutine:

```
Range("reference").
Name = "name"
```

Did you know?

Named ranges also appear in the Formula AutoComplete listings when you create a formula.

Did you know?

The name of the named range appears in the Name box, just above the headers for columns A and B.

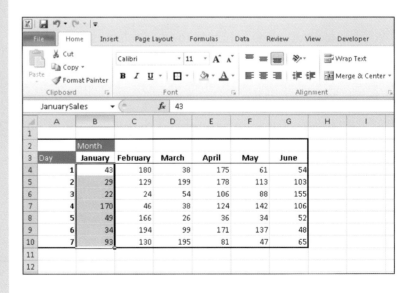

After you select a range, you might want to make the selection larger or smaller to fit the data it represents. For example, you might have a range with shipping rates for packages of differing weights. If your shipping agent adds or removes weight categories, you will need to resize the range to reflect the new information.

Using the `Resize` method, you can specify the number of rows and columns in the selected range. You can do that using the row size and column size arguments. The row size argument tells you how many rows should be encompassed by the selection, while the column size argument does the same for columns. The selection's definition starts from the existing top left cell of the range's definition and extends as far as the row size and column size parameters indicate. The general form of this method appears below:

```
Selection.Resize(rows, columns).Select
```

For example, you could have selected a small group of cells within a shipping rates schedule.

	A	B	C	D	E	F
1		Speed				
2	Region	7 Days	5 Days	3 Days	2 Day	Overnight
3	UK and Ireland	£ 5.00	£ 7.00	£ 15.00	£ 25.00	£ 40.00
4	Europe	£ 10.00	£ 12.00	£ 20.00	£ 30.00	£ 60.00
5	Asia and Pacific	£ 30.00	£ 50.00	£ 60.00	£ 70.00	£ 100.00
6	North America	£ 30.00	£ 50.00	£ 60.00	£ 70.00	£ 100.00
7	South America	£ 30.00	£ 50.00	£ 60.00	£ 70.00	£ 100.00

The following snippet demonstrates how to resize the selection so it is five rows by five columns in size:

```
Selection. Resize (5, 5)
```

	A	B	C	D	E	F
1		Speed				
2	Region	7 Days	5 Days	3 Days	2 Day	Overnight
3	UK and Ireland	£ 5.00	£ 7.00	£ 15.00	£ 25.00	£ 40.00
4	Europe	£ 10.00	£ 12.00	£ 20.00	£ 30.00	£ 60.00
5	Asia and Pacific	£ 30.00	£ 50.00	£ 60.00	£ 70.00	£ 100.00
6	North America	£ 30.00	£ 50.00	£ 60.00	£ 70.00	£ 100.00
7	South America	£ 30.00	£ 50.00	£ 60.00	£ 70.00	£ 100.00

Resize a selected range

6

Resize a selected range

1 Create a subroutine.

2 Enter code that uses the following pattern in the body of the subroutine:

```
Range ("name") .
Resize (RowSize :=
number, ColumnSize
:= number)
```

For your information

You must use one or both of the `RowSize` and `ColumnSize` parameters. If you leave either of them blank, Excel assumes they have a value of one.

For your information

The `RowSize` and `ColumnSize` parameters indicate the number of rows or columns in the new version of the range, not the rows or columns to be added or subtracted.

Set the column width

When you enter data into a worksheet column, Excel lets the data in a cell extend into empty cells to the right of the active cell. If the cells to the right of the active cell contain data, Excel displays those cells' contents instead. You can use VBA to find the width of a column or, if desired, change the column's width to a specific value. You can also use the **AutoFit** method to have Excel size the columns to display the entire contents of every cell in a column.

If your organisation has design standards you must follow when designing your worksheets, you can use VBA code to automate those settings. For example, if the committee producing your company's annual report requires that your worksheets have columns that are a specific width, you can open an approved version of the worksheet and use some of the code below to determine the width of a specific column and use that setting in your commands.

To determine the width of a column, you use the **Columns** collection's **Width** property. That property is read only, but you can change the width of a column using its **ColumnWidth** property. The following VBA code displays a column's width in points:

```
MsgBox("The column's width is " &
Columns(number).Width)
```

Set the column width

1. Create a subroutine.

2. Enter the following line of code to display the column's width in points:

   ```
   MsgBox("The
   column's width is "
   & Columns(number).
   Width)
   ```

3. Enter one of the following lines of code in the body of the subroutine to change the column's width:

   a. ```
      Columns(number).
      ColumnWidth =
      characters
      ```

   b. ```
      Columns(number).
      AutoFit
      ```

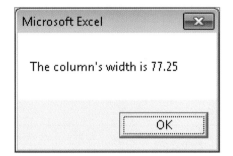

You can set the column width and characters using the following code:

```
Columns(number).ColumnWidth = characters
```

Did you know?

The **ColumnWidth** property is measured in characters, while the **Width** property is measured in points (1/72nds of an inch).

You can also use the **AutoFit** method to make a column wide enough to display the widest entry in its entirety. The section is equivalent to double-clicking on a column border in the column header bar. If a column contains data that is too long to fit in your worksheet columns as currently configured, using **AutoFit** is a reliable way to make your data more readable.

To invoke the **AutoFit** method, use the command:

```
Columns(number).AutoFit
```

Important

You refer to a column by number, not letter. For example, column D is column(4).

Set the row height

Set the row height

1. Create a subroutine.

2. Enter the following line of code in the subroutine to discover the row's height:

   MsgBox("The row's height is " & Rows(number). Height)

3. Enter the following line of code in the body of the subroutine to set the row's height:

   Rows(number). RowHeight = points

Just as you can measure and change the width of a column, you can do the same for your worksheet rows. Excel usually changes each row's height so it will display the tallest character it contains, but you might want to make each row a bit taller so there is some white space between rows of data. When done properly, adding white space makes your data much easier to read.

Like the **Columns** collection, the **Rows** collection stores a row's height in the **Height** property and lets you change the row's height by providing a new value for that property. The VBA code that displays a message box containing the row's height is:

```
MsgBox("The row's height is " &
Rows(number).Height)
```

and to set the height of row 1 to 24 points, the code is:

```
Rows(1).RowHeight = 24
```

Did you know?

In Excel 2010, rows are 15 points high by default.

Did you know?

Row height is measured in points, each point being 1/72nd of an inch.

Managing cells

Introduction

Every worksheet is divided into *cells*, which are boxes formed by the intersection of a row and column. You can manipulate the data in your worksheet's cells in many different ways, such as by cutting or copying data and pasting it elsewhere, managing cell comments, filling in sets of data automatically and finding and replacing values. Many of the techniques you will learn in this chapter should prove useful time and again.

Cut and paste a cell range

One of the more common tasks that you perform while using Excel is cutting data from one group of cells and pasting it into another. You can perform this task using Excel VBA, which speeds up the process considerably. As always, for the task to be repeatable, your worksheets must have predictable structures so the data you cut and paste will always end up in the right places.

The `Cut` method has one *required* parameter and one *optional* parameter. The required parameter is the address of the cell range to be cut. This range reference must identify a single, contiguous range of cells. For example, you could enter the following command to cut the range A2:C6:

```
Range ("A2:C6").Cut
```

You can also add a destination cell, which will serve as the top left cell in the range where Excel pastes the cells you cut. An example of a command that will do this would be:

```
Range("A2:C6").Cut Destination :=
Range("A12")
```

Cut and paste a cell range

1 Create a subroutine.

2 In the body of the subroutine, enter code that follows this pattern:

```
Range("address").
Cut Destination
:= Range("topleft
cell")
```

Did you know?

If you don't specify a `Destination` cell, this method cuts the data from the source cells and saves it on the Clipboard.

	A	B	C	D	E	F	G	H
1								
2								
3				March	April	May	June	
4				38	175	61	54	
5				199	178	113	103	
6				54	106	88	155	
7	4	170	46	38	124	142	106	
8	5	49	166	26	36	34	52	
9	6	34	194	99	171	137	48	
10	7	93	130	195	81	47	65	
11								
12		Month						
13	Day	January	February					
14	1	43	180					
15	2	29	129					
16	3	22	24					

Just as you can cut and paste cell data using Excel VBA, you can copy data and paste it into a destination range, too. The difference between *cutting* and copying is that *cutting* data from a cell range removes the data from the source cells, but *copying* it leaves the data in its original place while allowing you to paste a second copy into another group of cells.

Like the `Cut` method, the `Copy` method has one required parameter and one optional parameter. The required parameter is the address of the cell range to be copied. This range reference must identify a single, contiguous range of cells. For example, you could create the following command to copy the range A2:C7:

```
Range ("A2:C7").Copy
```

You can also add a destination cell to serve as the top left cell in the range where Excel pastes the cells you copied. An example of that command would be:

```
Range("A2:C7").Copy Destination :=
Range("A12")
```

▲	A	B	C	D	E	F	G	H
1								
2		Month						
3	Day	January	February	March	April	May	June	
4	1	43	180	38	175	61	54	
5	2	29	129	199	178	113	103	
6	3	22	24	54	106	88	155	
7	4	170	46	38	124	142	106	
8	5	49	166	26	36	34	52	
9	6	34	194	99	171	137	48	
10	7	93	130	195	81	47	65	
11								
12		Month						
13	Day	January	February					
14	1	43	180					
15	2	29	129					
16	3	22	24					
17	4	170	46					
18								

Copy and paste a cell ranges

Copy and paste a cell range

1 Create a subroutine.

2 In the body of the subroutine, enter code that follows this pattern:

```
Range("address").
Copy Destination
:= Range("topleft
cell")
```

Did you know?

If you don't use the optional **Destination** parameter, Excel copies the contents of the cell range to the Clipboard.

Important

This copy and paste command overwrites data in the target cells without alerting you it has done so.

Copy and paste values in cells using `PasteSpecial`

Copying and pasting data within Excel is a fairly straightforward process, both through the user interface and when using Excel VBA. You can have much more control over the paste operation by using `PasteSpecial`. For example, you can paste just the data and ignore the formatting in the original cell, apply the formatting of the target cell to the pasted data or use one of several other options to control how your pasted data appears.

Unlike copying and pasting a cell range, copying cell contents and using `PasteSpecial` to move them within a worksheet is a two-step process. The first step is the familiar one of copying the cells' contents to the clipboard. The second step is to use the **Range** object's `PasteSpecial` method to identify where and how the data should be pasted.

You identify which `PasteSpecial` operation Excel should use by selecting the appropriate **XlPasteType** variable. A list of the appropriate variables, which mirror the selections available in the Paste Special dialog box, appears in Table 7.1.

The following two lines of code copy the contents of the cell range A2:C7 and paste the values, without formatting, into the range starting with cell A9:

```
Range("A2:C7").Copy
Range("A9").PasteSpecial
Paste:=xlPasteValues
```

Copy and paste values in cells using `PasteSpecial`

1. Create a subroutine.

2. In the body of the subroutine, enter a command that follows this pattern:

```
Range("range").Copy

Range("topleft
cell").PasteSpecial
Paste:=XlPasteType
```

where:

a. `"range"` is the range from which you will copy the data.

b. `"topleftcell"` is the top left cell of the range into which you will paste the data.

c. `XlPasteType` is one of the variables listed in Table 7.1.

Jargon buster

You write **XlPasteType** with a capital 'X' to indicate that it represents a class of variables. Individual variables from the class, such as **xlPasteFormats**, are written with a lower-case 'x'.

	A	B	C	D	E	F	G	H
1								
2		Month						
3	Day	January	February	March	April	May	June	
4	1	43	180	38	175	61	54	
5	2	29	129	199	178	113	103	
6	3	22	24	54	106	88	155	
7	4	170	46	38	124	142	106	
8	5	49	166	26	36	34	52	
9	6	34	194	99	171	137	48	
10	7	93	130	195	81	47	65	
11								
12		Month						
13	Day	January	February					
14	1	43	180					
15	2	29	129					
16	3	22	24					
17	4	170	46					

Table 7.1 Available values for the `PasteSpecial` method's `XlPasteType` variable

Name	Description
`xlPasteAllExcept Borders`	Pastes all cell contents except borders
`xlPasteAllMerging ConditionalFormats`	Pastes all cell contents and merges conditional formats
`xlPasteAllUsing SourceTheme`	Pastes all cell contents and applies the Office Theme used to format the source cells
`xlPasteColumnWidths`	Applies the column widths of the pasted cells
`xlPasteComments`	Pastes comments from the source cells
`xlPasteFormats`	Pastes the formatting of the copied cells
`xlPasteFormulas`	Pastes formulas from the copied cells
`xlPasteFormulasAnd NumberFormats`	Pastes formulas and number formats of the copied cells
`xlPasteValidation`	Pastes validation rules from the copied cells
`xlPasteValues`	Pastes values from the copied cells
`xlPasteValuesAnd NumberFormats`	Pastes values and number formats from the copied cells

Important

You must use the `Copy` method to move the target cell range to the clipboard. If you use the `Cut` method, the `PasteSpecial` method will fail.

Transpose a column into a row

Transpose a column into a row

1 Create a subroutine.

2 In the body of the subroutine, enter code that follows this pattern:

```
Range("range").Copy

Range("topleft
cell").PasteSpecial
Transpose := True
```

where:

a. "range" is the range from which you will copy the data.

b. "topleftcell" is the top left cell of the range into which you will paste the data.

One often overlooked aspect of the Microsoft Excel worksheet is its primarily columnar nature. An Excel 2010 worksheet contains more than a million rows, but only several thousand columns. This design choice reflects the nature of business data. Columns tend to represent categories of data, such as a price or a model number, while rows tend to represent a complete set of data about business objects, such as orders or products. That said, you will occasionally need to transpose a column of data into a row or vice versa to fit your data into a target range.

To transpose a column into a row, you first use the **Range** object's **Copy** method to get the cell's contents onto the clipboard and then use the **PasteSpecial** method with its **Transpose** parameter set to **True**. So, to copy the values in cells B3:B10 and transpose those values into a row starting with cell A12, for example, the code would be:

```
Range("B3:B10").Copy
Range("A12").PasteSpecial
Transpose:=True
```

	A	B	C	D	E	F	G	H	I
1									
2		Month							
3	Day	January	February	March	April	May	June		
4		1	43	180	38	175	61	54	
5		2	29	129	199	178	113	103	
6		3	22	24	54	106	88	155	
7		4	170	46	38	124	142	106	
8		5	49	166	26	36	34	52	
9		6	34	194	99	171	137	48	
10		7	93	130	195	81	47	65	
11									
12	January	43	29	22	170	49	34	93	
13									

For your information

Note that the paste operation shown in the figure copied the borders and formatting from the original cells. You might need to reformat the destination cells.

Did you know?

You can also transpose data with *multiple* columns and rows. In that case, column 1 becomes row 1, column 2 becomes row 2 and so on.

When you design an Excel worksheet, you often have a very good sense of everything that's going on within it, even if you haven't examined the worksheet for a while. If you have to share a worksheet with a colleague or revisit a worksheet after several months, you might need some hints to remind yourself how everything works. One way that you can add that information to a worksheet is by creating cell comments.

When you use VBA to add a comment to a cell, you should first ensure the target cell contains no other comments. You can do so by invoking the **Cells** collection's **ClearComments** method. Once an existing cell's comments have been removed, calling the **AddComment** method followed by the text of the comment adds your annotation to the worksheet.

Within the **ClearComments** and **AddComment** method, you identify the target cell by its row and column. You use the row number as you would in any other command, but you must refer to the column by *number* instead of a *letter*. For example, E column is number 5, J is column 10 and so on. The following code samples show you how to clear comments from cell B4 and add a comment to the same cell:

```
Cells(4,2).ClearComments
Cells(4,2).AddComment ("Data changed on
13 July 2012.")
```

▲	A	B	C	D	E	F	G	H
1								
2		Month						
3	Day	January	February	March	April	May	June	
4	1	43	Curt: Data changed on 13 July 2012.		175	61	54	
5	2	29			178	113	103	
6	3	22			106	88	155	
7	4	170	46	50	124	142	106	
8	5	49	166	26	36	34	52	
9	6	34	194	99	171	137	48	
10	7	93	130	195	81	47	65	
11								

Create a cell comment

Create a cell comment

1 Create a subroutine.

2 In the body of the subroutine, enter code that follows this pattern:

```
Cells(row, column).
ClearComments

Cells(row, column).
Add Comment ("This
is the comment
text.")
```

7

Did you know?

A cell may contain at most one comment.

Important

Comments entered using VBA do not display an author's name, but Excel assigns the active user's name to the comment's **Author** property.

Display a cell's comment

Display a cell's comment

1 Create a subroutine and then do either of the following.

2 In the body of the subroutine, type code in the following pattern to display the comment in one cell:

```
Cells(row, column).
Comment.Visible =
True
```

3 Alternatively, enter code that follows this pattern to display all comments in a worksheet:

```
Dim c as Comment

For Each c In
ActiveSheet.
Comments

  c.Visible = True

Next
```

Did you know?

You can discover how many comments a worksheet contains by displaying the contents of the `Comments.Count` property.

If you haven't changed how Excel handles comments, then the program indicates that a cell contains a comment by displaying a small red flag at the top right corner of the cell. Those indicators can be a little difficult to see, especially if you're moving quickly, so you might want to display every comment within a worksheet to make it easier to find them.

To display an individual cell's comment, you identify the cell and then set the **Visible** property of its **Comment** object to **True**. The following line of code shows you how to do that for cell B4:

```
Cells(4,2).Comment.Visible = True
```

Setting a cell's **Comment.Visible** property to **True** is simple enough, but you do have to know that your target cell actually contains a comment. If you would rather display all comments within a worksheet, you can do so by moving through every member of a worksheet's **Comments** collection and setting each member's **Visible** property to **True**. The following sample code demonstrates the process required to display every comment in an active worksheet:

```
Dim c as Comment
For Each c In ActiveSheet.Comments
  c.Visible = True
Next
```

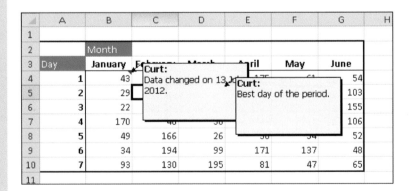

See also

For more information on using **For…Each** loops, see Chapter 12.

Cell comments make it easy to record information about your worksheets, both for yourself and for your colleagues. The disadvantage of cell comments is that they can take up a lot of room in your display and block your view of the data. If you have multiple comments open, it can take a while to close them all by hand. If you would like to close all of your comments at one time, you can do so from the user interface or by using Excel VBA.

To hide an individual cell's comment, you identify the cell and then set the `Visible` property of its `Comment` object to `False`. The following line of code shows you how to do that for cell C5:

```
Cells(5,3).Comment.Visible = False
```

Setting a cell's `Comment.Visible` property to `False` is simple enough, but you do have to know that your target cell actually contains a comment. If you would rather hide all comments within a worksheet, you can do so by moving through every member of a worksheet's `Comments` collection and setting each object's `Visible` property to `False`. The following sample code demonstrates the process required to display every comment in an active worksheet:

```
Dim c as Comment
For Each c In ActiveSheet.Comments
 c.Visible = False
Next
```

	A	B	C	D	E	F	G	H
1								
2		Month						
3	Day	January	February	March	April	May	June	
4	1	43	180	38	175	61	54	
5	2	29	129	199	178	113	103	
6	3	22	24	54	106	88	155	
7	4	170	46	38	124	142	106	
8	5	49	166	26	36	34	52	
9	6	34	194	99	171	137	48	
10	7	93	130	195	81	47	65	
11								

Did you know?

Even if you hide a comment, the red 'flag' indicator still appears in the top right corner of its cell.

Hide a cell's comment

Hide a cell's comment

1 Create a subroutine.

2 In the body of the subroutine, type code that follows this pattern to hide the comment in one cell:

```
Cells(row,column).
Comment.Visible =
False
```

3 Type code that follows this pattern to hide all comments in the worksheet:

```
Dim c as Comment
For Each c In
ActiveSheet.Comments
    c.Visible = False
Next
```

Did you know?

You must refer to a column by its number, not the letter that appears in the worksheet's column headers.

See also

For more information on `For...Each` loops, see Chapter 12.

Delete one or all cell comments

As you're developing an Excel worksheet, you might want to leave notes to yourself about why you took the steps you did to implement your solution. Cell comments are a wonderful way to do that. That said, notes to yourself might not be necessary after you are done editing your worksheet. If you find that you no longer need a comment, you can delete it.

To delete a comment, you identify the comment's cell by its row and column, then use the **Comment** object's **Delete** method to erase it. The command's general structure is as follows:

```
Cells(row, column).Comment.Delete
```

To delete the comment in cell B4, you would use the following line of code:

```
Cells(4,2).Comment.Delete
```

Note that you identify the row and column by number, even though columns are labelled using letters in the body of the worksheet.

You could delete every comment in a worksheet by moving through the **Comments** collection using a **For**...**Each** loop and using the **Delete** method for each member of the collection. The code to do that is:

```
Dim c as Comment
For Each c In ActiveSheet.Comments
  c.Delete
Next
```

Delete one or all cell comments

1 Create a subroutine.

2 In the body of the subroutine, enter code that follows this pattern to delete a cell's comment:

```
Cells(row, column).
Comment.Delete
```

3 Type code that follows this pattern to delete *all* comments in the worksheet:

```
Dim c as Comment
For Each c In
ActiveSheet.
Comments
  c.Delete
Next
```

Important

Deleting a comment using VBA can't be undone. Once it's deleted, it's gone for good.

See also

For more information on **For**...**Each** loops, see Chapter 12.

◢	A	B	C	D	E	F	G
1							
2		Month					
3	Day	January	February	March	April	May	June
4	1	43	180	38	175	61	54
5	2	29	129	199	178	113	103
6	3	22	24	54	106	88	155
7	4	170	46	38	124	142	106
8	5	49	166	26	36	34	52
9	6	34	194	99	171	137	48
10	7	93	130	195	81	47	65
11							

Entering data into an Excel worksheet can be a time-consuming, repetitive task. If the data you want to enter follows a specific pattern, such as a sequence of months or numbers that progress at a known rate, then you can fill a series of cells with those values using Excel's built-in data entry capabilities.

The **AutoFill** method has the following syntax:

```
Range ("source").AutoFill Destination:=
Range ("destination"), _
Type:=XlAutoFillType
```

The first range identifies the cells that contain the *source* of the data series, while the range identified in the **Destination** parameter identifies the range that will contain the series. The source range must be part of the destination range. For example, the following code snippet would extend the data series started in cells A10:A11 to cell A14:

```
Range ("A10:A11").AutoFill
Destination:=Range ("A10:A14")
```

9	Series
10	1
11	2
12	
13	
14	
15	

9	Series
10	1
11	2
12	3
13	4
14	5
15	

If cell A10 contained the number 1 and A11 the number 2, this code would extend the series to include the numbers 3, 4 and 5. Should you prefer another fill type, you can add the **Type** parameter to control how Excel extends the series. For example, the following command would extend the same series starting with the values 1 and 2 with 4, 8 and 16, due to the geometric growth trend:

```
Range ("A10:A11").AutoFill
Destination:=Range ("A10:A14"),
Type:=xlGrowthTrend
```

Fill a range of cells automatically

Fill a range of cells automatically   7

1 Create a subroutine.

2 In the body of the subroutine, enter code that follows this pattern:

3 `Range ("source"). AutoFill Destination:=Range ("destination")`

   a. If desired, type a comma followed by `Type:=XlAuto FillType`

   b. `XlAutoFillType` is a placeholder. You can select the fill type you want from the variables shown in Table 7.2.

Fill a range of cells automatically (cont.)

You'll find a full enumeration of the available fill types in Table 7.2.

Table 7.2 Available values for the `PasteSpecial` method's `XlAutoFillType` parameter

Name	Description
`xlFill Copy`	Copies values and formats from the selected cells to the target range, repeating values as required
`xlFill Days`	Extends a series of day names, copying formats and repeating values as required
`xlFill Default`	Fills values using Excel's built-in methodology for determining which values to include
`xlFill Formats`	Copies formats from the selected cells to the target range, repeating values as required
`xlFill Months`	Extends a series of month names, copying formats and repeating values as required
`xlFill Series`	Extends the values in the selected cells into the target range as a series (for example, '1, 2' is extended as '3, 4, 5') and copies formats from the selected cells, repeating as required
`xlFill Values`	Copies values from the selected cells to the target range, repeating values as required
`xlFill Weekdays`	Extends a series of work day names, copying formats and repeating values as required
`xlFill Years`	Extends a series of years, copying formats and repeating values as required
`xlGrowth Trend`	Extends a series of values based on multiplicative relationships (so '1, 2' would be extended as '4, 8, 16') and formats from the selected cells are copied and repeated as required
`xlLinear Trend`	Extends a series of values based on additive relationships (so '1, 2' would be extended as '3, 4, 5') and formats from the selected cells are copied and repeated as required

When you create worksheets within an Excel workbook, it's possible that you will want to create multiple copies of the same type of worksheet. For example, you might want to break out product sales by category for a series of months. If you have already entered those category labels into a worksheet, you can copy those values and paste them into multiple worksheets in one go.

In Excel VBA, you use the **Sheets** collection's **FillAcrossSheets** method to identify the source of the cell contents to be copied and the worksheets you want to copy those contents to. The **FillAcrossSheets** method is part of the **Sheets** collection, so you identify the sheets to which you want to copy the data and then provide the source range. The basic syntax of the **FillAcrossSheets** method follows this pattern:

```
Sheets(sArray).FillAcrossSheets
Worksheets("sheet name").Range("cells to
be copied")
```

- **sArray** is an array of worksheets to which you want to copy the cell contents named later in the code.

- **"sheet name"** is the name of the worksheet that contains the values to be copied.

- **copied range** is the range of cells to be copied.

An example of a properly constructed **FillAcrossSheets** method statement is this:

```
Dim sArray As Variant
sArray = Array("Sheet1", "Sheet2",
"Sheet3", "Sheet4")
Sheets(sArray).FillAcrossSheets
Worksheets("Sheet1").Range("D2:D8")
```

Did you know?

The **sArray** variable lists all of the worksheets you will use in your command.

Copy a range to multiple sheets

Copy a range to multiple sheets

7

1 Create a subroutine.

2 Enter code that follows this pattern in the body of the subroutine:

```
Dim sArray As
Variant
sArray =
Array("Sheet1",
"Sheet2", "Sheet3",
"Sheet4")
Sheets(sArray).
FillAcrossSheets
Worksheets("sheet").
Range("copied
range")
```

Important

!

One common error is to omit the source worksheet from the array, but, if you leave it out, the **FillAcrossSheets** method will fail.

Add a cell border

Excel worksheets store large amounts of data in a compact, easy-to-read format. That said, as worksheets get increasingly crowded, you might want to format some values, or labels, so they stand out from the remainder of the worksheet's contents. One way to do that is to add borders to a cell or cell range. Those borders make the values in the cell more prominent, which means they will be noticed more readily within the worksheet.

The command to add a border to a cell range calls the **Range** object's **BorderAround** method. In its most basic form, the command is quite straightforward:

```
Range("address").BorderAround
```

This version of the command adds a simple black border around the named cell range. You can change the characteristics of the border by specifying its **LineStyle**, **Weight** (thickness), **ColorIndex**, **Color** and **ThemeColor** parameters.

- **LineStyle** is the overall appearance of the line, such as continuous, dashed or dotted. A summary of available settings appears in Table 7.3.

- **Weight** is the thickness of the line. The four acceptable values appear in Table 7.4.

- **ColorIndex** indicates whether Excel should use the automatic colour (usually black) or no colour. The variables appear in Table 7.5.

- **Color** is an RGB value, such as (255, 255, 0) for yellow.

- **ThemeColor** is a list of the colours in the current theme. The acceptable variables for this parameter appear in Table 7.6.

You may only specify a value for *one* of the parameters **ColorIndex**, **Color** or **ThemeColor**. For example, you could create this statement:

```
Range("F7").BorderAround
LineStyle:=xlDot, Weight:=xlThick, _
Color:=RGB(255, 0, 0)
```

Add a cell border

1. Create a subroutine.

2. Enter code that follows this pattern in the body of the subroutine:

```
Range("address").
BorderAround
```

a. Add any of the parameters **LineStyle**, **Weight**, **ColorIndex**, **Color**, **ThemeColor**.

3. For more information on the values you can assign to the **BorderAround** method's parameters, see Tables 7.3, 7.4, 7.5 and 7.6.

◢	A	B	C	D	E	F
1		Speed				
2	Region	7 Days	5 Days	3 Days	2 Day	Overnight
3	UK and Ireland	£ 5.00	£ 7.00	£ 15.00	£ 25.00	£ 40.00
4	Europe	£ 10.00	£ 12.00	£ 20.00	£ 30.00	£ 60.00
5	Asia and Pacific	£ 30.00	£ 50.00	£ 60.00	£ 70.00	£ 100.00
6	North America	£ 30.00	£ 50.00	£ 60.00	£ 70.00	£ 100.00
7	South America	£ 30.00	£ 50.00	£ 60.00	£ 70.00	£ 100.00

Table 7.3 Values for `XlLineStyle` parameter in the `BorderAround` method

Name	Description
xlContinuous	Continuous line
xlDash	Dashed line
xlDashDot	Alternating dashes and dots
xlDashDotDot	Dash followed by two dots
xlDot	Dotted line
xlDouble	Double line
xlLineStyleNone	No line
xlSlantDashDot	Slanted dashes

Table 7.4 Values for `XlBorderWeight` parameter in the `BorderAround` method

Name	Description
xlHairline	Hairline (thinnest border)
xlMedium	Medium
xlThick	Thick (widest border)
xlThin	Thin

Table 7.5 Values for `XlColorIndex` parameter in the `BorderAround` method

Name	Description
xlColorIndexAutomatic	Automatic colour
xlColorIndexNone	No colour

Add a cell border (cont.)

? 7

Did you know?

If you change a workbook's Office Theme, you could alter the colour of borders for which you have specified a **ThemeColor** parameter value.

Add a cell border (cont.)

Table 7.6 Values for `XlThemeColor` parameter in the `BorderAround` method

Name	Description
`xlThemeColorAccent1`	Accent1
`xlThemeColorAccent2`	Accent2
`xlThemeColorAccent3`	Accent3
`xlThemeColorAccent4`	Accent4
`xlThemeColorAccent5`	Accent5
`xlThemeColorAccent6`	Accent6
`xlThemeColorDark1`	Dark1
`xlThemeColorDark2`	Dark2
`xlThemeColorFollowed Hyperlink`	Followed hyperlink
`xlThemeColorHyperlink`	Hyperlink
`xlThemeColorLight1`	Light1
`xlThemeColorLight2`	Light2

If you run a business, you might want to look up orders from a particular customer. For example, you might want to find the first order that a customer ever placed. You can use the built-in **Find** method to locate data of your choosing within your worksheets.

The **Find** method looks for the first occurrence of a target value in a specified cell range and activates the cell that contains the value. The **Find** method's syntax is:

```
Range ("range").Find(What:="term").
Activate
```

Activating the cell that contains the value you wanted to find indicates the value's presence within the body of the worksheet. You can then assign that cell's address to a variable using a command such as **strFound = ActiveCell.Address**.

If the **Find** method doesn't locate an instance of the **What** parameter's term, the method returns an error. You need to add error-handling code to your routine so your program doesn't halt. An example is:

```
On Error GoTo NoValue
Range ("A1:F7").Find(What:="Overnight").
Activate
Exit Sub
NoValue:
MsgBox ("The value doesn't occur within
the search range.")
```

Find a cell value

Find a cell value

1 Create a subroutine.

2 Enter code that follows this pattern in the body of the subroutine:

```
On Error GoTo
NoValue
Range ("range").
Find(What:="term").
Activate
Exit Sub
NoValue:
MsgBox ("The value
doesn't occur within
the search range.")
```

7

	A	B	C	D	E	F
1		Speed				
2	Region	7 Days	5 Days	3 Days	2 Day	Overnight
3	UK and Ireland	£ 5.00	£ 7.00	£ 15.00	£ 25.00	£ 40.00
4	Europe	£ 10.00	£ 12.00	£ 20.00	£ 30.00	£ 60.00
5	Asia and Pacific	£ 30.00	£ 50.00	£ 60.00	£ 70.00	£ 100.00
6	North America	£ 30.00	£ 50.00	£ 60.00	£ 70.00	£ 100.00
7	South America	£ 30.00	£ 50.00	£ 60.00	£ 70.00	£ 100.00

Find a cell value (cont.)

The first line tells Excel what to do if it encounters an error. Next, if the **Find** method does locate a cell with the target value, it activates that cell and, on the next line, exits the subroutine.

The next line is a label, **NoValue**, which provides a target for the **On Error** statement at the beginning of the code sample. Finally, the **MsgBox** line displays a box indicating that the value didn't occur within the search range. That line should be followed by an **End Sub** statement indicating the end of the subroutine.

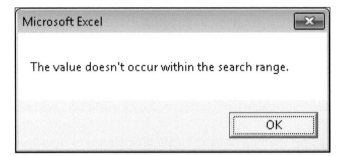

See also

For more information on handling errors in your VBA code, see Chapter 13.

Did you know?

You can use a variable's value as the target for the **What** parameter. If you do, you don't need to enclose the value in double quotes.

As the old saying goes, the only constant in life is change. If you want to replace a value within a worksheet, perhaps because a client moved or you have renamed product, you can do so using Excel's **Range** object's **Replace** method. The **Replace** method is the equivalent of the **Replace All** command you access via the user interface.

The **Replace** method requires three bits of information: the range to search within, the term to be replaced and the term with which to replace it. The basic syntax looks like this:

```
Range("range").Replace What:="term1",
Replacement:="term2"
```

An example of valid code that calls the **Replace** method would be:

```
Range("A1:F7").Replace
What:="Overnight", Replacement:="1 Day"
```

	A	B	C	D	E	F
1		Speed				
2	Region	7 Days	5 Days	3 Days	2 Day	Overnight
3	UK and Ireland	£ 5.00	£ 7.00	£ 15.00	£ 25.00	£ 40.00
4	Europe	£ 10.00	£ 12.00	£ 20.00	£ 30.00	£ 60.00
5	Asia and Pacific	£ 30.00	£ 50.00	£ 60.00	£ 70.00	£ 100.00
6	North America	£ 30.00	£ 50.00	£ 60.00	£ 70.00	£ 100.00
7	South America	£ 30.00	£ 50.00	£ 60.00	£ 70.00	£ 100.00

	A	B	C	D	E	F
1		Speed				
2	Region	7 Days	5 Days	3 Days	2 Day	1 Day
3	UK and Ireland	£ 5.00	£ 7.00	£ 15.00	£ 25.00	£ 40.00
4	Europe	£ 10.00	£ 12.00	£ 20.00	£ 30.00	£ 60.00
5	Asia and Pacific	£ 30.00	£ 50.00	£ 60.00	£ 70.00	£ 100.00
6	North America	£ 30.00	£ 50.00	£ 60.00	£ 70.00	£ 100.00
7	South America	£ 30.00	£ 50.00	£ 60.00	£ 70.00	£ 100.00

Replace a cell value

Replace a cell value

1 Create a subroutine.

2 Enter code that follows this pattern in the body of the subroutine:

```
Range("range").
ReplaceWhat:=
"term1",
Replacement:=
"term2"
```

Did you know?

The values for the **What** and **Replacement** parameters should be enclosed in double quotes, unless the values are passed to the method using variables.

Did you know?

Unlike the **Find** method, if the value in the **Replace** method's **What** parameter doesn't occur within the search range, the method does not generate an error.

Formatting worksheets and worksheet elements

Introduction

Individuals who create Microsoft Excel worksheets often spend a lot of time working on the logic of the worksheet, including formulas and summaries, so they can get the most out of their data. What they often overlook, unfortunately, is applying formatting that makes the data easier to read. In this chapter, you will learn how to apply formatting to your worksheets and individual cells using the facilities built into Excel VBA.

What you'll do

Apply bold, italic and underline formatting

Change a cell's font

Change a cell's font size

Change a cell's font colour

Change a cell's fill colour

Change a cell's alignment

Apply a cell style

Apply a number format to a cell

Clear a cell's format

Apply bold, italic and underline formatting

When you create a worksheet, you might want some cells' contents to stand out from the surrounding values. One of the most common ways to do that is to add formatting. You can make a cell's contents stand out by applying bold, italic or underline formatting.

The first step in applying any of these formats is to select the cell or cells using the **Range** object's **Select** method. This line of code shows how to select the range A3:B3:

```
Range("A3:B3").Select
```

After you select the cell range, you can apply formatting. To make a cell's contents bold, you set the selection's **Bold** property to **True**, as in the following example:

```
Selection.Font.Bold = True
```

Apply bold, italic and underline formatting

1. Create a subroutine.

2. In the body of the subroutine, type code that follows this pattern:

   **Range("address").
   Select**

3. Use any of the following commands to apply the desired formatting:

   **Selection.Font.Bold
   = True
   Selection.Font.
   Italic = True
   Selection.Font.
   Underline =
   XlUnderlineStyle**

Similarly, you set the **Italic** property to **True** to italicise the selection's contents:

```
Selection.Font.Italic = True
```

The **Underline** property operates differently than the **Bold** and **Italic** properties. Rather than set the **Underline** property's value to **True**, you need to assign it a value from the **XlUnderlineStyle** constant set. The four allowable underline styles are **xlUnderlineStyleSingle**, **xlUnderlineStyleDouble**, **xlUnderlineStyleDoubleAccounting** and **xlUnderlineStyleNone**, which turns underlining off.

The following line of code applies the standard single underline format to a selection:

```
Selection.Font.Underline =
xlUnderlineStyleSingle
```

As an example, suppose your worksheet contains data summarising orders.

	A	B	
1	Orders for June 15		
2			
3	Item	Destination	
4	Red Scarf	Loughsborough	
5	Blue Scarf	Manchester	
6	Fingerless Gloves	Chichester	
7	Drop Box	Swansea	
8			

If you apply the code noted above, the same worksheet would be formatted with bold, italic and a single underline applied to cells A3:B3.

	A	B	C
1	Orders for June 15		
2			
3	*Item*	*Destination*	
4	Red Scarf	Loughsborough	
5	Blue Scarf	Manchester	
6	Fingerless Gloves	Chichester	
7	Drop Box	Swansea	
8			

Did you know?

Setting either the **Bold** or **Italic** property to **False** turns off bold and italic text for the selected range.

Change a cell's font

The team that designed Microsoft Excel put a great deal of thought into choosing the font that best presents data in your worksheets. While that font makes your data easy to read, large or crowded worksheets can be difficult to comprehend because all of the text tends to look the same after a few moments. You can make portions of your worksheet, such as headers or totals, stand out by changing the font used to display those cells' contents.

Change a cell's font

1 Create a subroutine.

2 In the body of the subroutine, enter code that follows this pattern:

```
Range("range").
Select
Selection.Font.Name
= "font"
```

To change a cell's font using Excel VBA, you first select the cell range and then change the value assigned to the `Selection.Font.Name` property. The procedure uses two lines of code that follow this pattern:

```
Range("range").Select
Selection.Font.Name = "font"
```

For example, suppose you are presented with an order summary worksheet with a header in cell A1.

	A	B
1	Orders for June 15	
2		
3	*Item*	*Destination*
4	Red Scarf	Loughsborough
5	Blue Scarf	Manchester
6	Fingerless Gloves	Chichester
7	Drop Box	Swansea
8		

If you wanted to change the font of cell A1 to Cambria, you would use the following code:

```
Range("A1").Select
Selection.Font.Name = "Cambria"
```

Applying that code selects cell A1 and changes the font used to display its contents.

	A	B
1	Orders for June 15	
2		
3	*Item*	*Destination*
4	Red Scarf	Loughsborough
5	Blue Scarf	Manchester
6	Fingerless Gloves	Chichester
7	Drop Box	Swansea
8		

Did you know?

If you misspell the name of the font you want to apply, Excel VBA will not display an error even if there is no font of that name installed on your computer.

Important

The name of the font must be enclosed in double quotes.

Change a cell's font size

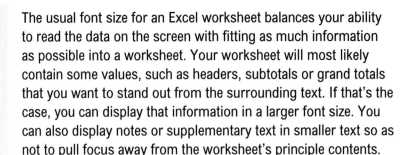

The usual font size for an Excel worksheet balances your ability to read the data on the screen with fitting as much information as possible into a worksheet. Your worksheet will most likely contain some values, such as headers, subtotals or grand totals that you want to stand out from the surrounding text. If that's the case, you can display that information in a larger font size. You can also display notes or supplementary text in smaller text so as not to pull focus away from the worksheet's principle contents.

To change the size of the text in a cell range, you first select the range using the **Range** object's **Select** method. The following line of code demonstrates the process for cell A1:

```
Range("A1").Select
```

	A	B
1	Orders for June 15	
2		
3	*Item*	*Destination*
4	Red Scarf	Loughsborough
5	Blue Scarf	Manchester
6	Fingerless Gloves	Chichester
7	Drop Box	Swansea
8		

After you have selected the target range, you can change the **Font** object's **Size** property to display the cell's contents at the desired size. Font sizes are measured in points – there are 72 points per inch. For example, changing a range's font size to 24 points would make the text $\frac{1}{3}$ of an inch in height. The following code does just that:

```
Selection.Font.Size = 24
```

	A	B
1	Orders for June 15	
2		
3	*Item*	*Destination*
4	Red Scarf	Loughsborough
5	Blue Scarf	Manchester
6	Fingerless Gloves	Chichester
7	Drop Box	Swansea
8		

Change a cell's font size

1 Create a subroutine.

2 In the body of the subroutine, enter code that follows this pattern:

```
Range("range").
Select
Selection.Font.Size
= number
```

? Did you know?

The default font size in Excel 2010 is 11 points.

Excel worksheets are terrific for organising and summarising data. The basic worksheet, however, is a rather bland mix of black, white and shades of grey. You can make your worksheets more visually interesting and make some values stand out from those around them by displaying a cell's contents in a colour other than black.

Changing a cell's font colour requires two lines of code. In the first step, you must select the cell range you want to affect. For example, you might have a worksheet with a header in cell A1.

	A	B
1	Orders for June 15	
2		
3	*Item*	*Destination*
4	Red Scarf	Loughsborough
5	Blue Scarf	Manchester
6	Fingerless Gloves	Chichester
7	Drop Box	Swansea
8		

To select cell A1, you would use the following line of code:

```
Range("A1").Select
```

After you have selected the range, you can use the **Font** object's **Color** property to assign a colour to the cell's text. The **Color** property defines colours using a mix of red, blue and green light, hence assigning it an RGB value. Each colour has an intensity from 0 to 255 and how they mix determines the final colour. For example, **RGB(0, 255, 0)** is pure green, while **RGB(255, 0, 0)** is pure red. Table 8.1 lists the RGB combinations for common colours.

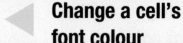

Change a cell's font colour

Change a cell's font colour

1 Create a subroutine.

2 In the body of the subroutine, enter code that follows this pattern:

```
Range("range").
Select
Selection.Font.Color
= RGB(red, green,
blue)
```

8

Table 8.1 Sample RGB values

Colour	Red value	Green value	Blue value
Black	0	0	0
Blue	0	0	255
Green	0	255	0
Cyan	0	255	255
Red	255	0	0
Magenta	255	0	255
Yellow	255	255	0
White	255	255	255

If you wanted to display the contents of cell A1 in blue, you would use the following code:

```
Selection.Font.Color = RGB(0, 0, 255)
```

	A	B
1	Orders for	June 15
2		
3	*Item*	*Destination*
4	Red Scarf	Loughsborough
5	Blue Scarf	Manchester
6	Fingerless Gloves	Chichester
7	Drop Box	Swansea
8		

Did you know?

You can find the RGB value for a specific colour by starting to record a macro, changing a cell's font to the colour and examining the code to see what value was recorded.

When you read data on the computer screen, the easiest colour scheme on the eyes is black text on a white or slightly off-white background. If you've ever visited a website with white text on a black background, you'll know how difficult it can be to read. Changing a cell's background – that is, its *fill colour* – makes that cell's contents stand out from the information around it.

As an example, your worksheet might contain a sample of orders placed on a given day. If your summary is divided into two columns, each column could have a header indicating the data contained within it.

	A	B
1	Orders for June 15	
2		
3	*Item*	*Destination*
4	Red Scarf	Loughsborough
5	Blue Scarf	Manchester
6	Fingerless Gloves	Chichester
7	Drop Box	Swansea
8		

To change the fill colour of the column header that appears in cells A3:B3, you could use the following code:

```
Range("A3:B3").Select
```

After you have selected the range, you can use the **Interior** object's **Color** property to assign the cells a background colour. The **Color** property defines colours using a mix of red, blue and green light. As noted in the previous section, each colour has an intensity from 0 to 255 and how they mix determines the final colour. For example, **RGB(0, 255, 0)** is pure green, while **RGB(255, 0, 0)** is pure red. Table 8.1, presented in the previous section, lists the RGB combinations for common colours.

Change a cell's fill colour

Change a cell's fill colour

1. Create a subroutine.

2. In the body of the subroutine, enter code that follows this pattern:

```
Range("range").
Select

Selection.Interior.
Color = RGB(red,
green, blue)
```

8

Change a cell's fill colour (cont.)

To fill the cells with a yellow background, you would use the command:

```
Selection.Font.Color = RGB(255, 255, 0)
```

◢	A	B
1	Orders for June 15	
2		
3	*Item*	*Destination*
4	Red Scarf	Loughsborough
5	Blue Scarf	Manchester
6	Fingerless Gloves	Chichester
7	Drop Box	Swansea
8		

See also

For RGB values of common colours, see Table 8.1 in the previous section.

For your information

A little colour goes a long way in a worksheet. Use it as a highlight, not a main feature.

When you enter data into an Excel worksheet, the program selects an alignment for your data. Text tends to start at the left and run to the right, so we say that data is left-aligned. Centred alignment works best for labels, while the right alignment is perfect for numbers. If you want to change a cell's alignment, you can use Excel VBA to do so.

As an example, you might have a worksheet that contains sales data for a single business day. The headers in cells A3:B3, which you could format using a different-coloured background and other formatting changes, will start with the same horizontal alignment as the rest of the text in your worksheet.

	A	B
1	Orders for June 15	
2		
3	*Item*	*Destination*
4	Red Scarf	Loughsborough
5	Blue Scarf	Manchester
6	Fingerless Gloves	Chichester
7	Drop Box	Swansea
8		

To change the alignment of cells A3:B3, you first select the cells using VBA code:

```
Select("A3:B3").Select
```

With the selection in place, you can change the value of the **Selection** object's **HorizontalAlignment** property to reflect the desired alignment. You can assign one of five constants to the **HorizontalAlignment** property – **xlCenter, xlDistributed, xlJustify, xlLeft** and **xlRight**.

Change a cell's alignment

Change a cell's alignment

1 Create a subroutine.

2 In the body of the subroutine, enter code that follows this pattern:

```
Range("range").
Select
Selection.
HorizontalAlignment
= alignment
```

where alignment is one of the following variables: **xlCenter, xlDistributed, xlJustify, xlLeft** and **xlRight**.

8

Change a cell's alignment (cont.)

The code to apply centred formatting to the cell would be:

```
Selection.HorizontalAlignment =
xlCenter.
```

	A	B
1	Orders for	June 15
2		
3	*Item*	*Destination*
4	Red Scarf	Loughsborough
5	Blue Scarf	Manchester
6	Fingerless Gloves	Chichester
7	Drop Box	Swansea

Did you know?

You can also set the **Selection. VerticalAlignment** property's value. Acceptable variables are **xlBottom**, **xlCenter**, **xlDistributed**, **xlJustify** and **xlTop**.

Formatting worksheet cells can take a lot of time when you have to remember the font, colours, size, alignment and other values applied to the cell. You can save all of those settings as a cell style and then apply the style with a few clicks on the user interface or a single command in Excel VBA.

You can display a list of styles available to you in a workbook by displaying the Home tab of the ribbon and then clicking the Styles gallery's More button. Doing so displays the full Styles gallery.

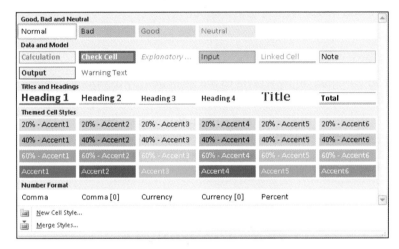

In most, but not all, cases, the style's name is the same as the label that appears in the gallery. You can find a style's proper name by hovering the mouse pointer over the style and reading the tool tip that appears.

Applying styles in VBA is a two-step process. The first step is to select the cell range you want to affect. As an example, suppose your worksheet has a heading in cell A1.

Important

Cell styles could change if you apply an Office Theme other than the one active when you applied the style.

Apply a cell style

1. Create a subroutine.

2. In the body of the subroutine, enter code that follows this pattern:

```
Range("range").
Select
Selection.Style =
"stylename"
```

8

Apply a cell style (cont.)

You can select A1 using this code:

```
Range("A1").Select
```

You can then apply a style to the selection by assigning the style's name to the **Selection** object's **Style** property. For example, the statement to format the selection using the **Title** style would look like this:

```
Selection.Style = "Title"
```

Entering numbers into your worksheet cells lets you view and summarise your data, but numerical data can be hard to read unless it's formatted properly. You can apply several built-in number formats using the `Selection` object's `Style` property.

To apply a number format to a cell range, you must first select the range using the `Range` object's `Select` method. For example, your worksheet might contain a list of VAT percentages in the cell range C4:C7.

	A	B	C
1	**Orders for June 15**		
2			
3	*Item*	*Destination*	*VAT (%)*
4	Red Scarf	Loughsborough	0.25
5	Blue Scarf	Manchester	0.25
6	Fingerless Gloves	Chichester	0.25
7	Drop Box	Swansea	0.25
8			

To select that cell range, you would use the following line of code:

```
Range("C4:C7").Select
```

With the selection in place, you can assign the name of the desired style to the Selection object's `Style` property. If you wanted to apply the Percent style, that command would be:

```
Selection.Style = "Percent"
```

	A	B	C
1	**Orders for June 15**		
2			
3	*Item*	*Destination*	*VAT (%)*
4	Red Scarf	Loughsborough	25%
5	Blue Scarf	Manchester	25%
6	Fingerless Gloves	Chichester	25%
7	Drop Box	Swansea	25%
8			

◀ Apply a number format to a cell

Apply a number format to a cell

1 Create a subroutine.

2 In the body of the subroutine, enter code that follows this pattern:

```
Range("range").
Select
Selection.Style =
"stylename"
```

where stylename is an existing style, the most commonly used ones being Number, Currency, Comma and Percent.

8

For your information

Some number formats have complicated definitions instead of a simple name. if you're not using one of the named formats shown above, you should consider recording a macro of you applying a number format and using the code Excel generates to change your cells.

Clear a cell's format

At times, the best format for a cell is the default format – one without embellishments, such as bold or italic type – and with the cell's contents presented in black text on a white background. If you have applied other formatting to a cell, you can remove it all with a straightforward VBA command.

For example, suppose your worksheet has a series of column labels with several types of formatting applied.

	A	B	C
1	Orders for June 15		
2			
3	*Item*	*Destination*	*VAT (%)*
4	Red Scarf	Loughsborough	25%
5	Blue Scarf	Manchester	25%
6	Fingerless Gloves	Chichester	25%
7	Drop Box	Swansea	25%

If you want to remove the formatting piece by piece, you would need to determine which formats you applied and then use the appropriate code to get rid of it. Instead, you can remove all formatting from a cell range by selecting the range and then using the `ClearFormats` method.

The VBA command to select a range relies on the `Range` object's `Select` method. To select cells A3:C3, you would use the following code:

```
Range ("A3:C3") .Select
```

With that selection in place, you need only invoke the `Selection` object's `ClearFormats` method to remove all formatting:

```
Selection.ClearFormats
```

Clear a cell's format

1. Create a subroutine.

2. In the body of the subroutine, enter code that follows this pattern:

```
Range ("range") .
Select
Selection.
ClearFormats
```

◢	A	B	C
1	**Orders for June 15**		
2			
3	Item	Destination	VAT (%)
4	Red Scarf	Loughsborough	25%
5	Blue Scarf	Manchester	25%
6	Fingerless Gloves	Chichester	25%
7	Drop Box	Swansea	25%
8			

If you want to apply specific formatting to a cell, such as bold and italic text (with no other changes), you should use the `ClearFormats` method first to remove any other formatting present in the cell.

?

Did you know?

Clearing a cell's format leaves the data intact, but will probably change how it's presented. This consideration is particularly true for dates.

8

Sorting and filtering data

Introduction

At times it can seem that Excel's ability to handle large data collections is actually a bad thing. Even small home-based businesses can generate large amounts of data, making it difficult to process your worksheets quickly. One of the best ways to focus on the data that is most important to you at the moment is to sort and filter the data within a worksheet. The Sorting feature displays all of your data, arranging it in a more meaningful order, while filters temporarily limit what data is displayed in your worksheet.

If you want to create a complex sort or filter, such as one that uses multiple values and affects multiple columns, you should strongly consider recording a macro of you creating the filter via the user interface. Be sure that the code you record affects the data list you want the macro to work on or else change the macro so that it does. Doing so will save you a lot of time.

Note: Some of the lines of code in this chapter are too long for the page to accommodate. In Excel VBA, you can type a space and then an underscore character (_) to indicate that the current command continues on the next line. For example:

```
ActiveWorkbook.Worksheets("Sheet1").
Sort.SortFields.Add _
   Key:=Range("B4"), Order:=xlDescending
```

What you'll do

Sort cell data using a single criterion

Create a multilevel sort

Sort using a customised list of values

Turn on filter arrows using VBA code

Apply a filter using a single criterion

Remove a filter

Display a list of unique values

Filter data to display two values in a column

Filter data to display three or more values in a column

Filter data based on values in multiple columns

Sort cell data using a single criterion

The data you enter into your Excel worksheets will most likely have an inherent order. For home-based businesses, the most common orders are based on time. When you capture sales for a month, a week or a day, the data you enter will reflect that structure. If you want to arrange your worksheet based on some other information you collect, you can do so by sorting your data.

To sort your data using VBA, it should be arranged as a list with column headers and no blank rows in the body of the list. That is because a blank row indicates the end of a list, so any data below the blank row would not be included in the sort operation.

	A	B	C
1	**Sales for January**		
2			
3	Day	Sales	
4	1	£ 141.00	
5	2	£ 767.00	
6	3	£ 571.00	
7	4	£ 282.00	
8	5	£ 210.00	
9	6	£ 243.00	
10	7	£ 706.00	
11	8	£ 296.00	
12	9	£ 650.00	
13	10	£ 592.00	
14	11	£ 428.00	
15	12	£ 150.00	
16	13	£ 169.00	
17	14	£ 781.00	

Sorting data using VBA is a multistep process. The first step is to activate a cell within the data list using the **Range** object's **Activate** method, replacing the range with the address of a cell in the data list:

```
Range("range").Activate
```

Next, it is usually a good idea to clear any other sort operations that have been applied to the data list. Even though most single-criterion sort operations will affect your data in a predictable way, you can do this by using the following command, replacing **sheet_name** with the actual name of the worksheet:

```
ActiveWorkbook.Worksheets("sheet_name").
Sort.SortFields.Clear
```

After clearing all existing sorting operations from a range, you can initiate a new sort. For example, you can sort the data in a range in descending order, based on the values in a key cell's column. The general syntax for that statement would be:

```
ActiveWorkbook.Worksheets("sheet_name").
Sort.SortFields.Add _
   Key:=Range("cell"), Order:=XlSortOrder
```

The **XlSortOrder** constant can be either **xlDescending**, to sort in descending order, or **xlAscending**, to sort in ascending order.

With those commands in place, you can initiate the sort operation. The standard pattern for the next sequence uses the **With…End With** construction, which lets you streamline your references to multiple members of an object. The code's pattern is as follows:

```
With ActiveWorkbook.Worksheets("sheet_
name").Sort
   .SetRange Range("range")
   .Header = xlNo or xlYes
   .Apply
End With
```

As a concrete example, suppose you want to sort data in the range A4:B34 based on the values in column B, with the column B values sorted in descending order. To do so, you would use the following code:

See also

For more information on the **With…End With** construction, see Chapter 12.

Sort cell data using a single criterion (cont.)

```
Range("B4").Activate
ActiveWorkbook.Worksheets("Sheet1").
Sort.SortFields.Clear
ActiveWorkbook.Worksheets("Sheet1").
Sort.SortFields.Add _
  Key:=Range("B4"), Order:=xlDescending
With ActiveWorkbook.Worksheets
("Sheet1").Sort
  .SetRange Range("A4:B34")
  .Header = xlNo
  .Apply
End With
```

After you have run this routine, your data will have changed order, to reflect its new, sorted order.

◢	A	B	C
1	Sales for January		
2			
3	Day	Sales	
4	14	£ 781.00	
5	2	£ 767.00	
6	18	£ 736.00	
7	31	£ 723.00	
8	7	£ 706.00	
9	30	£ 692.00	
10	16	£ 681.00	
11	29	£ 660.00	
12	9	£ 650.00	
13	22	£ 626.00	
14	10	£ 592.00	

Sort cell data using a single criterion

1. Create a subroutine.

2. In the body of the subroutine, type code that follows this pattern:

```
Range("B4").Activate
ActiveWorkbook.Worksheets("Sheet1").
Sort.SortFields.Clear
ActiveWorkbook.Worksheets("Sheet1").
Sort.SortFields.Add Key:=Range("B4"), _
   Order:=xlDescending
With ActiveWorkbook.
Worksheets("Sheet1").Sort
   .SetRange Range("A4:B34")
   .Header = xlNo
   .Apply
End With
```

Sort cell data using a single criterion (cont.)

Did you know?

You can streamline creating a sort operation by recording a macro of you sorting data and then modifying the VBA code to meet your needs.

9

Create a multilevel sort

Rearranging your data can help you discover important information about your business. If you offer several types of products for sale, you might be interested in finding out which months have the best sales for each of those products. To discover that information, you could create a multilevel sort that organises your data first by product and then by month.

Implementing a multilevel sort in Excel VBA is exactly the same as implementing a single-level sort, with the addition of a second statement identifying a sort field, the range to which it applies and the order into which Excel should sort the range's values. The code to add a sort field follows this pattern:

```
ActiveWorkbook.Worksheets("sheet_name").
Sort.SortFields.Add _
Key:=Range("range"), Order:=XlSortOrder
```

The order in which the sort commands appear in your code is the order in which the sort criteria will be applied to your data. For example, you could sort sales data by month and then by value or by value and then by month.

The overall pattern for sorting a data list based on values in two columns is to clear any existing sorts, define the two sort key fields, then implement the sort using the **With**...**End With** construction to simplify your code. The first line of code clears all existing sort operations from a worksheet:

```
ActiveWorkbook.Worksheets("sheet_name").
Sort.SortFields.Clear
```

Next, you define sort operations for each of the columns you want to sort:

```
ActiveWorkbook.Worksheets("sheet_name")
.Sort.SortFields.Add _
  Key:=Range("col_range1"),
  Order:=xlAscending
ActiveWorkbook.Worksheets("sheet_name")
.Sort.SortFields.Add _
  Key:=Range("col_range2"),
  Order:=xlDescending
```

Finally, you use the **With**...**End With** construction to apply the sort operation:

```
With ActiveWorkbook.Worksheets("sheet_
name").Sort
   .SetRange Range("range")
   .Header = xlYes or xlNo
   .Apply
End With
```

As an example, you might have a set of data in cells A3:C12, including column headers.

	A	B	C
1	**Sales by Category**		
2			
3	**Month**	**Category**	**Sales**
4	January	Boxes	£ 126.00
5	February	Boxes	£ 485.00
6	March	Boxes	£ 188.00
7	January	Gloves	£ 146.00
8	February	Gloves	£ 219.00
9	March	Gloves	£ 179.00
10	January	Scarves	£ 423.00
11	February	Scarves	£ 138.00
12	March	Scarves	£ 175.00

To sort the data by product category and then by sales, you could use the following VBA code:

```
ActiveWorkbook.Worksheets("Sheet2").
Sort.SortFields.Clear
ActiveWorkbook.Worksheets("Sheet2").
Sort.SortFields.Add _
   Key:=Range("B4:B12"),
   Order:=xlAscending
ActiveWorkbook.Worksheets("Sheet2").
Sort.SortFields.Add _
   Key:=Range("C4:C12"),
   Order:=xlDescending
```

9

```
With ActiveWorkbook.
Worksheets("Sheet2").Sort
   .SetRange Range("A3:C12")
   .Header = xlYes
   .Apply
End With
```

After you run the code, your data will be in the following order.

◢	A	B	C
1	**Sales by Category**		
2			
3	**Month**	**Category**	**Sales**
4	February	Boxes	£ 485.00
5	March	Boxes	£ 188.00
6	January	Boxes	£ 126.00
7	February	Gloves	£ 219.00
8	March	Gloves	£ 179.00
9	January	Gloves	£ 146.00
10	January	Scarves	£ 423.00
11	March	Scarves	£ 175.00
12	February	Scarves	£ 138.00

Create a multilevel sort

1 Create a subroutine.

2 In the body of the subroutine, enter code that follows this pattern:

```
ActiveWorkbook.Worksheets
("sheet_name").Sort.SortFields.Clear
```

Next, you define sort operations for each of the columns you want to sort.

```
ActiveWorkbook.Worksheets("sheet_name")
.Sort.SortFields.Add Key:=Range("col_
range1"), _
   Order:=xlAscending
```

```
ActiveWorkbook.Worksheets("sheet_name")
.Sort.SortFields.Add Key:=Range("col_
range2"), _
   Order:=xlDescending
```

Finally, you use the **With**...**End With** construction to apply the sort operation:

```
With ActiveWorkbook.Worksheets("sheet_
name").Sort
    .SetRange Range("range")
    .Header = xlYes or xlNo
    .Apply
End With
```

For your information

The **Sort** method affects the unbroken block of cells that includes the ranges named in the **SortFields**. **Add** lines of code.

9

Sort using a customised list of values

Microsoft Excel recognises several ways to sort your data. It can sort by number, alphabetical order, as well as a customised list of values that you define. Customised lists give you a great deal of control over how you present your data within your Excel worksheets, which makes them very useful when you analyse your data. The program includes a number of built-in custom lists, such as month and weekday names, but you can define your own custom lists as part of the VBA sort code.

As an example, suppose you have a data set summarising category sales by month, with the original data list sorted by month and then by category. Note that the categories appear in alphabetical order.

	A	B	C
1	**Sales by Category**		
2			
3	**Month**	**Category**	**Sales**
4	January	Boxes	£ 126.00
5	January	Gloves	£ 146.00
6	January	Scarves	£ 423.00
7	February	Boxes	£ 485.00
8	February	Gloves	£ 219.00
9	February	Scarves	£ 138.00
10	March	Boxes	£ 188.00
11	March	Gloves	£ 179.00
12	March	Scarves	£ 175.00

Sorting worksheet data using VBA is a multistep process. Your first step should be to clear all sort fields that have been applied to your worksheet. Doing so ensures your data will be sorted consistently, starting from the data's original order. You use the following code to clear all sort operations from a worksheet:

```
ActiveWorkbook.Worksheets("sheet_name").
Sort.SortFields.Clear
```

Next, you can define a sort order for a column of data. You can create a customised list to sort values in a specific column. For example, you could sort the list by category based on the order 'Gloves, Scarves, Boxes'. To define that list as part of a sort operation, you would use the following code:

**Sort using a
customised list
of values (cont.)**

```
ActiveWorkbook.Worksheets("sheet_name").
Sort.SortFields.Add _
    Key:=Range("col_range"),
    Order:=XlSortOrder, _
    CustomOrder:="item1, item2, item3…"
```

The previous statement requires that you enter the name of the worksheet, the column of cells that contain the values to be sorted, whether to sort the values in **xlAscending** or **xlDescending** order and the list of customised values by which to sort.

After you have defined the sort operation, you apply it using the **Sort** object's methods. As per usual, you can streamline your code by using the **With…End With** code construction.

```
With ActiveWorkbook.Worksheets("sheet_
name").Sort
    .SetRange Range("range")
    .Header = xlYes or xlNo
    .Apply
End With
```

In the previous code, you replace **sheet_name** with the name of the worksheet that contains the data to be sorted, **range** with the full range of data to be affected, use **xlYes** or **xlNo** to indicate whether or not the list has column headers and call the **Apply** method to invoke the operation.

The full code to sort data on Sheet2, in the cell range A3:C12, based on values in B4:B12, would be:

```
Range("B4").Select
ActiveWorkbook.Worksheets("Sheet2").
Sort.SortFields.Clear
ActiveWorkbook.Worksheets("Sheet2").
```

9

Sort using a customised list of values (cont.)

```
Sort.SortFields.Add _
  Key:=Range("B4:B12"),
  Order:=xlAscending, _
  CustomOrder:="Gloves, Scarves, Boxes"
With ActiveWorkbook.Worksheets
("Sheet2").Sort
  .SetRange Range("A3:C12")
  .Header = xlYes
  .Apply
End With
```

	A	B	C
1	**Sales by Category**		
2			
3	**Month** ▼	**Category** ↓↑	**Sales** ▼
4	January	Gloves	£ 146.00
5	February	Gloves	£ 219.00
6	March	Gloves	£ 179.00
7	January	Scarves	£ 423.00
8	February	Scarves	£ 138.00
9	March	Scarves	£ 175.00
10	January	Boxes	£ 126.00
11	February	Boxes	£ 485.00
12	March	Boxes	£ 188.00

As with other sorting operations, you might find it easier to record a macro of you creating the sort and replay it when required. If you use an existing customised list in your sort, Excel records the values in the macro code.

Sort using a customised list of values

1 Create a subroutine.

2 In the body of the subroutine, enter code that follows this pattern:

```
Range("cell").Select
ActiveWorkbook.Worksheets("sheet_
name").Sort.SortFields.Clear
ActiveWorkbook.Worksheets("sheet_name")
.Sort.SortFields.Add Key:=Range("col_
range"), _
   Order:=XlSortOrder, CustomOrder:=
   "item1, item2, item3…"
With ActiveWorkbook.Worksheets("sheet_
name").Sort
   .SetRange Range("full_range")
   .Header = xlYes or xlNo
   .Apply
End With
```

Sort using a customised list of values (cont.)

For your information

The list items in the `CustomOrder` parameter are case-sensitive. If your customised sorting order doesn't work properly, ensure the terms are properly capitalised.

Did you know?

If the column you sort using a custom values contains entries that aren't in the list, those rows will appear at the bottom of the sorted list.

9

Turn on filter arrows using VBA code

Turn on filter arrows using VBA code

1 Create a subroutine.

2 In the body of the subroutine, enter code that follows this pattern:

```
Range("cell").
Activate
Selection.
AutoFilter
```

One of Excel's greatest strengths is its ability to handle large amounts of data quickly and efficiently. Of course, that is also a bit of a disadvantage. Worksheets that contain large data collections can be hard to analyse. Fortunately, you can limit the data that appears in your worksheet by applying filters. The first step is to turn on filter arrows.

To turn on filter arrows for a data list, you activate any cell in the list and then use the `Selection` object's `AutoFilter` method to display the filter arrows. The code pattern looks like this:

```
Range("cell").Activate
Selection.AutoFilter
```

To give a specific example, let's assume your data list summarises monthly sales by category.

	A	B	C
1	**Sales by Category**		
2			
3	**Month**	**Category**	**Sales**
4	February	Gloves	£ 219.00
5	March	Gloves	£ 179.00
6	January	Gloves	£ 146.00
7	February	Boxes	£ 485.00
8	March	Boxes	£ 188.00
9	January	Boxes	£ 126.00
10	January	Scarves	£ 423.00
11	March	Scarves	£ 175.00
12	February	Scarves	£ 138.00

If you know cell B4 will always be in the data list you want to filter, you could use the following code to display the filter arrows:

```
Range("B4").Activate
Selection.AutoFilter
```

When run, the filter arrows then appear at the top of the data list that includes cell B4.

▲	A	B	C
1	**Sales by Category**		
2			
3	**Month** ▾	**Category** ▾	**Sales** ▾
4	February	Gloves	£ 219.00
5	March	Gloves	£ 179.00
6	January	Gloves	£ 146.00
7	February	Boxes	£ 485.00
8	March	Boxes	£ 188.00
9	January	Boxes	£ 126.00
10	January	Scarves	£ 423.00
11	March	Scarves	£ 175.00
12	February	Scarves	£ 138.00

If filter arrows have *already* been applied to a data range, running the `Selection.AutoFilter` code statement will turn them off.

?

Did you know?

Excel applies filter arrows to the top row of the current region, so it's best to have column headers atop your lists.

9

Apply a filter using a single criterion

Excel filters limit the data that appears in a worksheet. In VBA, the process of applying a filter consists of two steps: turning on filter arrows if they are off and then identifying the range, field and criterion used to limit the data displayed in your worksheet.

To apply a filter to a range, you call the **Range** object's **AutoFilter** method. The AutoFilter method has two parameters:

- **Field** – the number of the column by which you want to filter the list.

- **Criteria1** – the term that must appear in the target field for the row to appear in the filtered list.

The syntax of an **AutoFilter** method follows this pattern:

```
ActiveSheet.Range("range").AutoFilter
Field:=field_no,Criteria1:="term"
```

As an example, suppose you have a data list summarising monthly sales for different categories of products. The three fields are named 'Month', 'Category' and 'Sales'.

Apply a filter using as single criterion

1. Create a subroutine.

2. In the body of the subroutine, enter code that follows this pattern:

```
ActiveSheet.Range
("$A$3:$C$12").
AutoFilter
Field:=2,
Criteria1:="Gloves"
```

	A	B	C
1	**Sales by Category**		
2			
3	**Month** ▾	**Category** ▾	**Sales** ▾
4	February	Gloves	£ 219.00
5	March	Gloves	£ 179.00
6	January	Gloves	£ 146.00
7	February	Boxes	£ 485.00
8	March	Boxes	£ 188.00
9	January	Boxes	£ 126.00
10	January	Scarves	£ 423.00
11	March	Scarves	£ 175.00
12	February	Scarves	£ 138.00

The `AutoFilter` method statement to display only those rows that contain the term 'Gloves' in the second field is:

```
ActiveSheet.Range("$A$3:$C$12").
AutoFilter Field:=2, _
   Criteria1:="Gloves"
```

Running a subroutine with that statement would display only those rows that contain the word 'Gloves' in the 'Category' column.

	A	B	C
1	**Sales by Category**		
2			
3	Month ▾	Category ▾	Sales ▾
4	February	Gloves	£ 219.00
5	March	Gloves	£ 179.00
6	January	Gloves	£ 146.00

Did you know?

Filter arrows must be turned on for the code listed above to work.

Jargon buster

If your data is laid out so that each column represents a fact, such as a product name or sales amount, then a field is the same as a column. In this case, `Field:=2` represents the second column in the data list.

9

Remove a filter

Filters are extremely useful things, but you will certainly want to remove them from time to time. When you're ready to remove a filter, all you need to do is identify the range of cells to which the filter is applied – that is, the column within the data list – and then leave the filter argument blank. Doing so sets the filter to blank and so allows all values to be displayed.

As an example, suppose you start with a data list that has been filtered based on values in the second column.

Remove a filter

1 Create a subroutine.

2 In the body of the subroutine, enter code that follows this pattern:

```
ActiveSheet.
Range("range").
AutoFilter
Field:=field_no
```

To remove a filter from a range, you call the **Range** object's **AutoFilter** method and use the **Field** parameter to identify the column, or field, from which to remove the filter. The syntax of the statement is:

```
ActiveSheet.Range("range").AutoFilter
Field:=field_no
```

The **AutoFilter** statement to remove the filter from the second field in a list spanning cells A3:C12 in the active worksheet is:

```
ActiveSheet.Range("$A$3:$C$12").
AutoFilter Field:=2
```

Running a subroutine with that statement would remove the filter from the 'Category' column and restore the data list to its original display.

	A	B	C
1	**Sales by Category**		
2			
3	**Month** ▾	**Category** ▾	**Sales** ▾
4	February	Gloves	£ 219.00
5	March	Gloves	£ 179.00
6	January	Gloves	£ 146.00
7	February	Boxes	£ 485.00
8	March	Boxes	£ 188.00
9	January	Boxes	£ 126.00
10	January	Scarves	£ 423.00
11	March	Scarves	£ 175.00
12	February	Scarves	£ 138.00

!

Important

Removing a filter using VBA is a one-way action, meaning you can't click the Undo toolbar button and reapply the filter.

9

Display a list of unique values

Some of the more interesting information you can discover about your data comes from identifying unique values in a list. For example, you might be interested in seeing how many different customers ordered from you in the past month, but not be that concerned about the total amount ordered by any one customer.

For example, you might have a data list summarising orders by month and category.

	A	B	C
1	**Sales by Category**		
2			
3	**Month** ↴	**Category** ↴	**Sales** ▾
4	January	Boxes	£ 126.00
5	January	Gloves	£ 146.00
6	January	Scarves	£ 423.00
7	February	Boxes	£ 485.00
8	February	Gloves	£ 219.00
9	February	Scarves	£ 138.00
10	March	Boxes	£ 188.00
11	March	Gloves	£ 179.00
12	March	Scarves	£ 175.00

You use the `Range` object's `AdvancedFilter` method to display a list of unique values in a data list. The `AdvancedFilter` method requires three pieces of information to display unique values only:

■ `Range` – the column of cells you want to inspect for unique values.

■ `Action` – whether a filter of the list is in place or to copy the cells to a destination range.

■ `Unique` – controls whether or not the filter should display rows that contain the first occurrence of each unique value in the range.

The basic syntax of the **AdvancedFilter** method, when used to identify unique values in a column, is:

```
Range("range").AdvancedFilter
Action:=xlFilterInPlace, Unique:=True
```

Because you want to display unique values, the **Action** and **Unique** parameter values won't change. The only information you need to provide is the range of cells representing the column by which you want to filter the list. If you want to filter the 'Category' column, that range is B3:B12, so the full **AdvancedFilter** statement would be:

```
Range("B3:B12").AdvancedFilter
Action:=xlFilterInPlace, Unique:=True
```

When you run a subroutine that contains this **AdvancedFilter** statement the result would contain three rows, representing the first occurrence of the differing values in cells B3:B12.

	A	B	C
1	**Sales by Category**		
2			
3	Month	Category	Sales
4	January	Boxes	£ 126.00
5	January	Gloves	£ 146.00
6	January	Scarves	£ 423.00

Display a list of unique values

1 Create a subroutine.

2 In the body of the subroutine, enter code that follows this pattern:

```
Range("range").AdvancedFilter Action:=
xlFilterInPlace, Unique:=True
```

Display a list of unique values (cont.)

9

?

Did you know?

When you filter a list so it only displays unique values, copying and pasting the list puts just the visible values in the destination cells.

Filter data to display two values in a column

So far, you've learned how to create simple filters for your Excel data, but Excel is capable of applying complex and powerful filters. As you might expect, the next step up is to display results corresponding with two values in your list. For example, you might want to see sales results for the months of January and February or two classes of products.

For example, suppose you want to filter a data list to display all rows that contain either the word 'Boxes' or 'Gloves' in the second column.

	A	B	C
1	**Sales by Category**		
2			
3	**Month**	**Category**	**Sales**
4	January	Boxes	£ 126.00
5	January	Gloves	£ 146.00
6	January	Scarves	£ 423.00
7	February	Boxes	£ 485.00
8	February	Gloves	£ 219.00
9	February	Scarves	£ 138.00
10	March	Boxes	£ 188.00
11	March	Gloves	£ 179.00
12	March	Scarves	£ 175.00

The command to filter a column so it displays rows that contain either of two values follows this pattern:

```
ActiveSheet.Range("range").AutoFilter
Field:=field_no, _
  Criteria1:="=term1", Operator:=xlOr,
Criteria2:="=term2"
```

where:

- **Range** is the entire cell range to be filtered
- **Field** is the column in the data list to be searched for the named values

Did you know?

The **Criteria1** and **Criteria2** arguments are a holdover from when you could only filter a list using two values.

- **Criteria1** is the first term to look for, with the term enclosed in quotes and preceded within the quotes by an equals sign

- **Operator** is the logical operator used to indicate either **Criteria1** or **Criteria2** may occur, so it will always be **xlOr**

- **Criteria2** is the second term to look for, with the term enclosed in quotes and preceded within the quotes by an equals sign.

So:

```
ActiveSheet.Range("$A$3:$C$12").
AutoFilter Field:=2, _
    Criteria1:="=Boxes", Operator:=xlOr,
Criteria2:="=Gloves"
```

Running a subroutine containing this code would filter a data list so it displays just those rows containing either the value 'Boxes' or 'Gloves' in the second column.

	A	B	C
1	**Sales by Category**		
2			
3	**Month** ▾	**Category** ⊤	**Sales** ▾
4	January	Boxes	£ 126.00
5	January	Gloves	£ 146.00
7	February	Boxes	£ 485.00
8	February	Gloves	£ 219.00
10	March	Boxes	£ 188.00
11	March	Gloves	£ 179.00

Filter data to display two values in a column (cont.)

Filter data to display two values in a column

1 Create a subroutine.

2 In the body of the subroutine, enter code that follows this pattern:

```
ActiveSheet.
Range("range").
AutoFilter
Field:=field_
no,Criteria1:=
"=term1", _

Operator:=xlOr,
Criteria2:="=term2"
```

9

See also

For more information on filtering a list using more than two values, see the next task.

Filter data to display three or more values in a column

Filter data to display three or more values in a column

1 Create a subroutine.

2 In the body of the subroutine, enter code that follows this pattern:

```
ActiveSheet.
Range("range").
AutoFilter
Field:=field_no,
Criteria1:=Array( _
"term1", "term2"…)
Operator:
=xlFilterValues
```

If you've created Excel filters via the user interface, you have probably created filters where you select a series of three or more values from those present in the column. Two-value filters use the rather archaic method of identifying `Criteria1` and `Criteria2` in the body of the VBA code. If you want to create a filter for three or more values, you can identify the values you want to display in an array.

For example, suppose you have a data list summarising product sales by month.

	A	B	C
1	**Sales by Category**		
2			
3	**Month**	**Category**	**Sales**
4	January	Boxes	£ 126.00
5	January	Gloves	£ 146.00
6	January	Scarves	£ 423.00
7	February	Boxes	£ 485.00
8	February	Gloves	£ 219.00
9	February	Scarves	£ 138.00
10	March	Boxes	£ 188.00
11	March	Gloves	£ 179.00
12	March	Scarves	£ 175.00
13	March	Flats	£ 204.00
14	March	Aprons	£ 301.00

If you want to display just those rows that contain sales figures for 'Boxes', 'Flats', 'Gloves' and 'Scarves', you could create a filter using the **Range** object's **AutoFilter** method. These statements have the following syntax:

```
ActiveSheet.Range("range").AutoFilter
Field:=field_no, _
Criteria1:=Array("term1", "term2",
"term3"…), _
Operator:=xlFilterValues
```

where:

- **Range** is the entire cell range to be filtered

- **Field** is the column in the data list to be searched for the named values

- **Criteria1** contains an array with a list of values to be displayed when the filter is applied, each term being enclosed in quotation marks

- **Operator** is the logical operator used to indicate that Excel should filter the list based on an array of values – as such, it's value will always be **xlFilterValues** for this type of operation.

The code to filter a list to display rows that contain the values 'Boxes', 'Flats', 'Gloves' and 'Scarves' would be:

```
ActiveSheet.Range("$A$3:$C$14").
AutoFilter Field:=2, Criteria1:=Array( _
"Boxes", "Flats", "Gloves", "Scarves"),
Operator:=xlFilterValues
```

Applying this filter would modify the data list so it would not display the row containing data about 'Aprons' sales.

	A	B	C
1	**Sales by Category**		
2			
3	**Month** ▾	**Category** ⊤	**Sales** ▾
4	January	Boxes	£ 126.00
5	January	Gloves	£ 146.00
6	January	Scarves	£ 423.00
7	February	Boxes	£ 485.00
8	February	Gloves	£ 219.00
9	February	Scarves	£ 138.00
10	March	Boxes	£ 188.00
11	March	Gloves	£ 179.00
12	March	Scarves	£ 175.00
13	March	Flats	£ 204.00
15			

Important

Excel treats all values in filter criteria, even numbers, as strings of characters, so you must enclose each of the array entries in double quotes.

Filter data based on values in multiple columns

Filter data based on values in multiple columns

1. Create a subroutine.

2. In the body of the subroutine, enter code that follows this pattern:

```
ActiveSheet.
Range ("range").
AutoFilter
Field:=column_1,
Criteria1:="term1"

ActiveSheet.
Range ("range").
AutoFilter
Field:=column_2,
Criteria1:="term2"
```

Previously, all of the filters you've learned have been based on the values in a single column. If you want, you can create a filter rule for any or all of the columns in your data list. All you need to do is determine which values and rules you want to use and apply them.

To apply multiple filters to a range, you call the **Range** object's **AutoFilter** method for each column by which you want to filter the list. The **AutoFilter** method has two parameters:

- **Field** – the number of the column by which you want to filter the list.

- **Criteria1** – the term that must appear in the target field for the row to appear in the filtered list.

The syntax of an **AutoFilter** method follows this pattern:

```
ActiveSheet.Range ("range").AutoFilter
Field:=field_no, Criteria1:="term"
```

You need to create separate statements for each column by which you want to filter your data. As an example, suppose you have a data list summarising monthly sales for different categories of products. The three fields are named 'Month', 'Category' and 'Sales'.

	A	B	C
1	**Sales by Category**		
2			
3	**Month**	**Category**	**Sales**
4	January	Boxes	£ 126.00
5	January	Gloves	£ 146.00
6	January	Scarves	£ 423.00
7	February	Boxes	£ 485.00
8	February	Gloves	£ 219.00
9	February	Scarves	£ 138.00
10	March	Boxes	£ 188.00
11	March	Gloves	£ 179.00
12	March	Scarves	£ 175.00

If you want the list to display just those results for 'Gloves' sales in January, you would run a subroutine containing the following code:

```
ActiveSheet.Range("$A$3:$C$12").
AutoFilter Field:=2, Criteria1:="Gloves"
ActiveSheet.Range("$A$3:$C$12").
AutoFilter Field:=1,Criteria1:="January"
```

The filters combine to reduce the list to the only row that contains the term 'January' in the first column and 'Gloves' in the second.

	A	B	C
1	**Sales by Category**		
2			
3	**Month** 🔽	**Category** 🔽	**Sales** 🔽
5	January	Gloves	£ 146.00
13			

?

Did you know?

Applying consecutive filters to the same field, such as filtering Field 1 for January and then for February, displays the results of the last filter you apply.

Filter data based on values in multiple columns (cont.)

9

Managing charts

Introduction

One of the real strengths of Excel 2010 is its ability to summarise large amounts of data. You can create formulas, tables and even pivot tables to manipulate your data set to discover important facts about your organisation and its operations.

As with all things, a strength can also turn out to be, if not a weakness, a challenge. Humans have a hard time keeping track of large data sets in their heads. It's all well and good to look at the summary, but if you create a pivot table that spans multiple screens, even the best summary operations will only help so much.

You can make your data easy to comprehend by summarising it visually using charts. In Excel 2010, you can use VBA to define and format your charts, which include the new sparkline chart type. *Sparklines* are designed for use in dashboards and other compact reporting applications, which fit well with Excel 2010's positioning as a reporting tool for all levels of an organisation.

Note: Some of the lines of code in this chapter are too long for the page to accommodate. In Excel VBA, you can type a space and then an underscore character (_) to indicate that the current command continues on to the next line.

What you'll do

Create a chart

Move a chart to a chart sheet

Add a new data series to a chart

Format a chart's legend text

Format a chart's axis text

Export a chart as an image

Create a Line sparkline

Create a Column sparkline

Create a Win/Loss sparkline

Delete a sparkline

Create a chart

When you are ready to summarise your Excel data visually, you can create a chart. To do this, you need just three lines of code. The first line of code calls the **Charts** collection's **Add** method:

```
ActiveSheet.Shapes.AddChart.Select
```

With the chart in place, you can now define the chart's type. To do that, you set a value for the **ActiveChart** object's **ChartType** property. The line of code you use follows this pattern:

```
ActiveChart.ChartType = XlChartType
```

The **XlChartType** constant refers to one of many available chart types, identified by constants within the **XlChartType** collection. Table 10.1 lists the **XlChartType** constants for common chart types.

Table 10.1 XlChartType values for commonly used chart types

Type	XlChartType value	Description
Area	xlArea	Area chart
Column (clustered)	xlColumnClustered	Clustered column chart (the default chart type)
Stacked column	xlColumnStacked	A stacked column chart
Line	xlLine	A line chart
Line with markers	xlLineMarkers	A line chart with markers for each data point
Pie	xlPie	A pie chart
XY scatter	xlXYScatter	A scatter chart (also called an XY chart)

Finally, you need to identify the range that provides the data for your chart. You can do that by calling the **ActiveChart** object's **SetSourceData** method, which includes the **Source** parameter. You set the parameter's value to the range that contains the data you want to appear in your chart. The general syntax for the **SetSourceData** method is this:

```
ActiveChart.SetSourceData
Source:=Range("range")
```

Here's an example to show you the code in use. Suppose you want to create a clustered column chart to summarise monthly sales for your company. Your worksheet might contain two columns of data.

	A	B
1	**Sales for the Year**	
2		
3	**Month**	**Sales**
4	January	£ 1,000.00
5	February	£ 1,275.00
6	March	£ 1,400.00
7	April	£ 942.00
8	May	£ 1,185.00
9	June	£ 1,468.00
10	July	£ 1,995.00
11	August	£ 702.00
12	September	£ 1,503.00
13	October	£ 1,474.00
14	November	£ 2,590.00
15	December	£ 4,025.00

You can create a clustered column chart based on this data using the following three lines of code:

```
ActiveSheet.Shapes.AddChart.Select
ActiveChart.ChartType = XlChartType
ActiveChart.SetSourceData Source:=Range
"Sheet1!$A$3:$B$15")
```

10

Create a chart (cont.)

Running this code against the data set creates a clustered column chart.

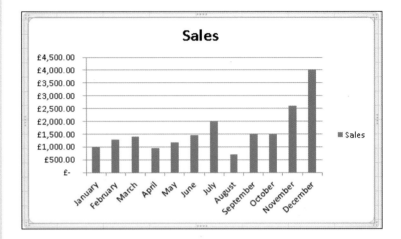

Create a chart

1. Create a subroutine.

2. In the body of the subroutine, type code that follows this pattern:

```
ActiveSheet.Shapes.
AddChart.Select
ActiveChart.
ChartType =
XlChartType
ActiveChart.
SetSourceData
Source:=Range
("range")
```

When you create a chart using VBA code, Excel creates the chart on the sheet that contains the data. The chart your code creates is large enough to display all of the data, but it is still relatively small in comparison to the size of the worksheet. Moving a chart to its *own* chart sheet ensures the chart will take up the entire sheet, making it more legible and easier to comprehend. This consideration is especially true for users viewing your content on a mobile device.

Suppose you create a chart that resides on the same worksheet as the data used create it.

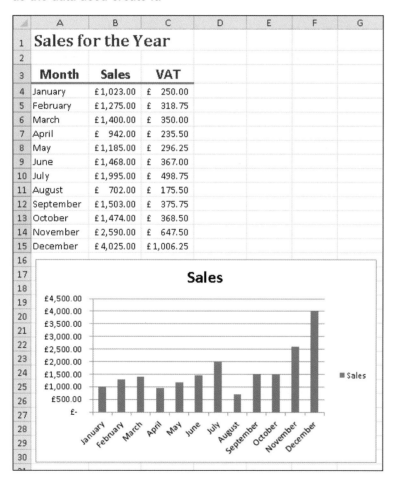

Move a chart to a chart sheet (cont.)

The first step to moving a chart to a chart sheet is it to select the chart. The VBA code to do that is:

```
ActiveChart.ChartArea.Select
```

After you select the chart, you need to exit Excel's cut and copy mode. You're probably familiar with cut and copy mode from when you cut and paste worksheet contents from one range to another. When you select the cells and then press either Ctrl+X or Ctrl+C, Excel surrounds your selected cells with a marquee. The *marquee* indicates that cut and copy mode is on. To exit cut and copy mode from the keyboard, you press the Esc key. In VBA, the command to exit cut and copy mode is:

```
Application.CutCopyMode = False
```

With the chart selected and cut and copy mode off, you can move it to a new sheet. You do that using the **ActiveChart** object's **Location** property, by means of which you assign a value to the **Where** parameter. To move your chart to a new sheet, you use the following VBA command:

```
ActiveChart.Location
Where:=xlLocationAsNewSheet
```

Running these three lines of code as part of the subroutine moves the chart from a worksheet to its own chart sheet.

> **Jargon buster**
>
> The **Application.CutCopyMode = False** statement changes the workbook from cut and copy mode to edit mode. The program does the same thing when you cut or copy workbook cells and paste them in your workbook. Cut and copy mode is on (**"True"**) when your cells are surrounded by a dotted line; cut and copy mode is off (**"False"**) when the dotted line is replaced by a solid outline.

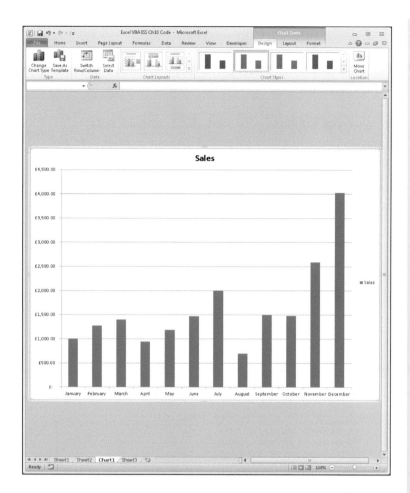

Move a chart to a chart sheet

1. Create a subroutine.

2. In the body of the subroutine, enter code that follows this pattern:

```
ActiveChart.
ChartArea.Select

Application.
CutCopyMode = False

ActiveChart.Location
Where:=xlLocation
AsNewSheet
```

! Important

This routine assumes you have just one chart on the active sheet.

10

Add a new data series to a chart

Charts summarise data you collect, whether about your business, organisation or leisure activities. If you create a chart and want to add more data to the summary, you can do so using Excel VBA.

For example, suppose your worksheet contains data summarising a monthly sales and VAT for a given year, but your chart only displays the sales data.

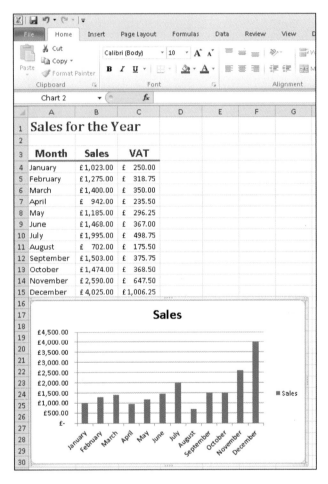

You can add the data for the VAT collected to your chart quickly using Excel VBA. A sequence of related data that is plotted within a chart is called a *data series*. For example, sales data for the months January to December might appear in cells B4:B15, with the series title, 'Sales', appearing in B3. The data series for VAT collected has its title in cell C3 and the data in cells C4:C15.

The VBA code required to add a data series to a chart starts by selecting the active chart's chart area:

```
ActiveChart.ChartArea.Select
```

After you select the chart you want to work with, you create a new series by calling the **Series** collection object's **NewSeries** method. The code for that action is quite straightforward:

```
ActiveChart.SeriesCollection.NewSeries
```

Now that you have added a new series to the chart's **Series** collection, you need to give the series a name. In most cases, you will want to use the column label from the worksheet data list as the series name. You assign a data series a name using the following code:

```
ActiveChart.SeriesCollection(series_no).
Name = "=formula"
```

The **series_no** value represents the new data series' position in the **SeriesCollection** object. You determine that value by counting the number of existing data series in your chart and add one. The **=formula** value is a formula that identifies a cell from which to draw the value or the value itself.

Finally, you must identify the cell range that contains the series values. The VBA statement to make that assignment uses the **SeriesCollection** object's **Values** property and is very similar to the code used to identify the series' name.

```
ActiveChart.SeriesCollection(series_no).
Values = "=range"
```

In the VBA code used to assign the range for the **Values** property, the **=range** variable is an equal sign followed by a range reference of the form **sheet_name!range**, such as **=Sheet1!$B$2:$B$5**.

10

The sequence of statements used to add a series with its name in cell C3 of Sheet2 and its values in the range C4:C15 of the same sheet would be:

```
ActiveChart.ChartArea.Select
ActiveChart.SeriesCollection.NewSeries
ActiveChart.SeriesCollection(2).Name =
"=Sheet2!$C$3"
ActiveChart.SeriesCollection(2).Values =
"=Sheet2!$C$4:$C$15"
```

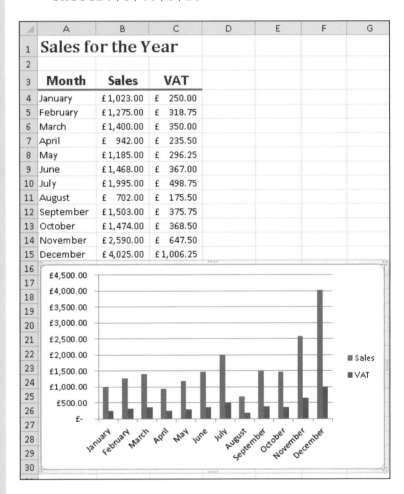

Add a new data series to a chart

1 Create a subroutine.

2 In the body of the subroutine, enter code that follows this pattern:

```
ActiveChart.ChartArea.Select
ActiveChart.SeriesCollection.NewSeries
ActiveChart.SeriesCollection
 (series_no).Name = "=formula"
ActiveChart.SeriesCollection
 (series_no).Values = "=range"
```

?

Did you know?

You can discover the number of data series in your chart by displaying the chart's legend and counting the number of entries it lists.

10

Format a chart's legend text

When you create a chart in Excel 2010, the program formats your chart legend's text in a default font.

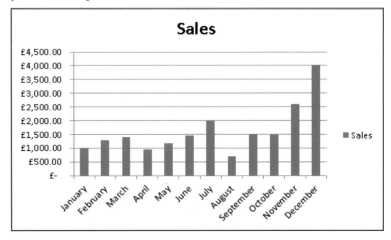

If your company's style sheet or your personal aesthetic calls for a different font, you can change the legend's font easily. To change the font of a chart's legend text, you must first select the chart and then the legend using these commands:

```
ActiveChart.ChartArea.Select
ActiveChart.Legend.Select
```

You then select the text frame that contains the legend's text, identify the text range and reference the **Font** property. You should use a **With...End With** code construct to streamline your code significantly.

```
With Selection.Format.TextFrame2.
TextRange.Font
  .NameComplexScript = "font"
  .NameFarEast = "font"
  .Name = "font"
End With
```

You set the **NameComplexScript**, **NameFarEast** and **Name** properties to reflect the new font so your chart will display properly for all users, regardless of their local language settings. This level of detail might seem excessive, but it is helpful in an international business environment.

The code to change the font of the chart legend's text to Arial is as follows:

```
ActiveChart.ChartArea.Select
ActiveChart.Legend.SelectWith Selection.
Format.TextFrame2.TextRange.Font
   .NameComplexScript = "Arial"
   .NameFarEast = "Arial"
   .Name = "Arial"
End With
```

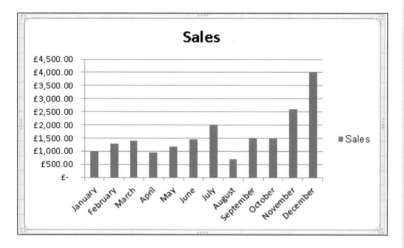

Format a chart's legend text

1️⃣ Create a subroutine.

2️⃣ In the body of the subroutine, enter code that follows this pattern:

```
ActiveChart.ChartArea.Select
ActiveChart.Legend.Select
With Selection.Format.TextFrame2.
TextRange.Font
   .NameComplexScript = "font"
   .NameFarEast = "font"
   .Name = "font"
End With
```

For your information

The code in this task assumes the chart is selected in the worksheet before you run the macro.

For your information

Some chart types might not store their legend text in the **TextFrame2** object. If the specific macro code listed above doesn't work for a specific chart, record a macro of you changing that chart's legend text formatting and use it as the base for your procedure.

10

Format a chart's axis text

When you create a chart in Excel 2010, the program formats your chart's axis labels using a default font.

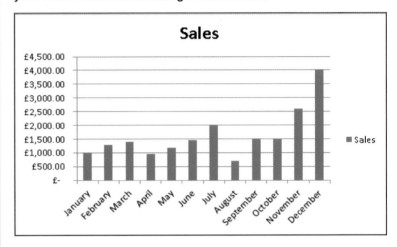

If you would prefer a different font, you can change it easily. To change the font of a chart's axis label text, you must first select the legend using these commands:

```
ActiveChart.ChartArea.Select
ActiveChart.Axes(XlAxis).Select
```

The first command selects the chart, while the second command uses the **Axes** property and looks at the **XlAxis** variable to determine which axis to select. You refer to the vertical axis using the **xlValue** variable and the horizontal axis using the **xlCategory** variable.

You then select the text frame that contains the axis label's text, identify the text range and reference the **Font** property. You should use a **With...End With** code construct to streamline your code significantly.

```
With Selection.Format.TextFrame2.
TextRange.Font
  .NameComplexScript = "font"
  .NameFarEast = "font"
  .Name = "font"
End With
```

You set the **NameComplexScript**, **NameFarEast** and **Name** properties to reflect the new font so your chart will display properly for all users, regardless of their local language settings. Making these changes ensures your chart will appear as desired in an international business environment.

The code to change the font of the chart's horizontal axis text to Tahoma would be as follows:

```
ActiveChart.ChartArea.Select
ActiveChart.Axes(xlCategory).Select
With Selection.Format.TextFrame2.
TextRange.Font
   .NameComplexScript = "Tahoma"
   .NameFarEast = "Tahoma"
   .Name = "Tahoma"
End With
```

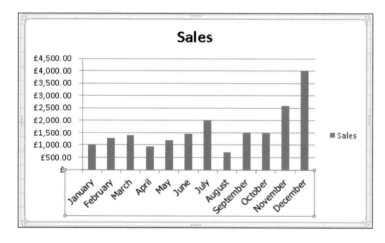

Format a chart's axis text

1. Create a subroutine.

2. In the body of the subroutine, enter code that follows this pattern:

```
ActiveChart.ChartArea.Select
ActiveChart.Axes(XlAxis).Select
With Selection.Format.TextFrame2.
TextRange.Font
   .NameComplexScript = "font"
   .NameFarEast = "font"
   .Name = "font"
End With
```

For your information

Some chart types might not store their axis label text in the **TextFrame2** object. If the specific macro code listed above doesn't work for a specific chart, record a macro of you changing that chart's axis label text formatting and use it as the base for your procedure.

10

Export a chart as an image

When you create a chart in Excel 2010, the program establishes a link between the chart and its data source. Any time the data source changes, Excel updates the chart to reflect the change. This feature is extremely useful for dashboards and other data summaries that should be updated whenever the data changes, but it is less useful for charts that draw data from files stored on a network that might be temporarily unavailable.

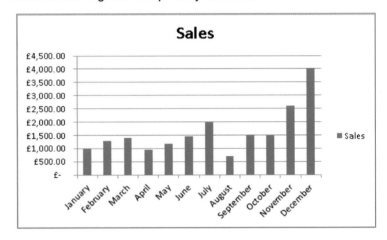

If you want to export an image of a chart's current appearance, you can do so by copying the chart's chart area and then pasting it into a destination cell range as an image. Copying the chart area requires this single line of code, which assumes the chart you want to copy has already been clicked:

```
ActiveChart.ChartArea.Copy
```

You then select the cell range where you want to paste the chart image and implement the paste operation. Pasting the image on the same worksheet takes these two lines of code:

```
Range("range").Select
ActiveSheet.Pictures.Paste.Select
```

If you want to paste the image on to another worksheet, you must activate that worksheet using the **Sheets.Activate** method. For example, the command to activate a worksheet named Sheet2 would be:

```
Sheets("Sheet2").Activate
```

The **range** variable is a reference to a cell range. If you paste the image on to the same worksheet, you do not need to specify the sheet's name. If you want to paste the image on another worksheet, or even another workbook, though, you need to provide that information as well.

For example, the following code would paste a chart as an image on Sheet2 in cell A1:

```
ActiveChart.ChartArea.Copy
Sheets("Sheet2").Activate
Range("Sheet2!$A$1").Select
ActiveSheet.Pictures.Paste.Select
```

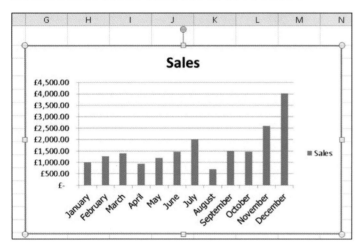

Export a chart as an image

1 Create a subroutine.

2 In the body of the subroutine, enter code that follows this pattern:

```
ActiveChart.ChartArea.Copy

Range("range").Select

ActiveSheet.Pictures.Paste.Select
```

Did you know?
Running the **ActiveChart.ChartArea.Copy** code copies the chart's image to the clipboard. You can then paste the image into any other file, not just the active Excel workbook.

10

Create a Line sparkline

One of the more useful aspects of Excel 2010 has been the introduction of sparklines. Sparklines, invented by Edward Tufte, are word-sized graphics that convey information normally communicated using a full-sized chart.

Several different types of sparklines are available to you in Excel 2010. For example, suppose you have a data set summarising monthly sales, VAT, your sales targets for each month and how the results compare with that target.

	A	B	C	D	E
1	**Sales for the Year**				
2					
3	**Month**	**Sales**	**VAT**	**Target**	**Result**
4	January	£ 1,023.00	£ 250.00	£ 750.00	£ 273.00
5	February	£ 1,275.00	£ 318.75	£ 1,200.00	£ 75.00
6	March	£ 1,400.00	£ 350.00	£ 1,400.00	£ -
7	April	£ 942.00	£ 235.50	£ 1,000.00	-£ 58.00
8	May	£ 1,185.00	£ 296.25	£ 1,000.00	£ 185.00
9	June	£ 1,468.00	£ 367.00	£ 1,200.00	£ 268.00
10	July	£ 1,995.00	£ 498.75	£ 1,750.00	£ 245.00
11	August	£ 702.00	£ 175.50	£ 1,000.00	-£ 298.00
12	September	£ 1,503.00	£ 375.75	£ 1,500.00	£ 3.00
13	October	£ 1,474.00	£ 368.50	£ 1,500.00	-£ 26.00
14	November	£ 2,590.00	£ 647.50	£ 2,500.00	£ 90.00
15	December	£ 4,025.00	£ 1,006.25	£ 4,000.00	£ 25.00

One way to summarise this data is to create a Line sparkline, which is an extremely compact line chart. To create a Line sparkline using VBA, you first identify the target cell where you want the sparkline to appear. Next, you call the **SparklineGroups** object's **Add** method and specify both the type of sparkline and the source of the sparkline's data.

The syntax of the statement to create a Line sparkline is:

```
Range("targetrange").SparklineGroups.Add
Type:=xlSparkLine, SourceData:="source"
```

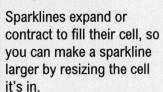

Did you know?

Sparklines expand or contract to fill their cell, so you can make a sparkline larger by resizing the cell it's in.

The `Type` parameter takes the value `xlSparkLine` to signify a Line sparkline, while the `SourceData` parameter specifies the cell range supplying the sparkline's data. For example, you might create a Line sparkline in cell E1 using data from cells B4:B15:

```
Range("E1").SparklineGroups.Add
    Type:=xlSparkLine, SourceData:="B4:B15"
```

◢	A	B	C	D	E
1	**Sales for the Year**				～⁄
2					
3	**Month**	**Sales**	**VAT**	**Target**	**Result**
4	January	£ 1,023.00	£ 250.00	£ 750.00	£ 273.00
5	February	£ 1,275.00	£ 318.75	£ 1,200.00	£ 75.00
6	March	£ 1,400.00	£ 350.00	£ 1,400.00	£ -
7	April	£ 942.00	£ 235.50	£ 1,000.00	-£ 58.00
8	May	£ 1,185.00	£ 296.25	£ 1,000.00	£ 185.00
9	June	£ 1,468.00	£ 367.00	£ 1,200.00	£ 268.00
10	July	£ 1,995.00	£ 498.75	£ 1,750.00	£ 245.00
11	August	£ 702.00	£ 175.50	£ 1,000.00	-£ 298.00
12	September	£ 1,503.00	£ 375.75	£ 1,500.00	£ 3.00
13	October	£ 1,474.00	£ 368.50	£ 1,500.00	-£ 26.00
14	November	£ 2,590.00	£ 647.50	£ 2,500.00	£ 90.00
15	December	£ 4,025.00	£ 1,006.25	£ 4,000.00	£ 25.00

Create a Line sparkline

1 Create a subroutine.

2 In the body of the subroutine, enter code that follows this pattern:

```
Range("targetrange").SparklineGroups.
Add Type:=xlSparkLine, _
SourceData:="source"
```

10

Create a Column sparkline

Excel 2010 is an exceptionally useful reporting tool. You can create dashboards that provide overviews of your organisation's data at a glance. Sparklines, which are compact charts that fit within a single worksheet cell, help convey that information effectively.

Several different types of sparklines are available to you. For example, suppose you wanted to summarise monthly sales using a Column sparkline.

	A	B	C	D	E
1	**Sales for the Year**				
2					
3	**Month**	**Sales**	**VAT**	**Target**	**Result**
4	January	£ 1,023.00	£ 250.00	£ 750.00	£ 273.00
5	February	£ 1,275.00	£ 318.75	£ 1,200.00	£ 75.00
6	March	£ 1,400.00	£ 350.00	£ 1,400.00	£ -
7	April	£ 942.00	£ 235.50	£ 1,000.00	-£ 58.00
8	May	£ 1,185.00	£ 296.25	£ 1,000.00	£ 185.00
9	June	£ 1,468.00	£ 367.00	£ 1,200.00	£ 268.00
10	July	£ 1,995.00	£ 498.75	£ 1,750.00	£ 245.00
11	August	£ 702.00	£ 175.50	£ 1,000.00	-£ 298.00
12	September	£ 1,503.00	£ 375.75	£ 1,500.00	£ 3.00
13	October	£ 1,474.00	£ 368.50	£ 1,500.00	-£ 26.00
14	November	£ 2,590.00	£ 647.50	£ 2,500.00	£ 90.00
15	December	£ 4,025.00	£ 1,006.25	£ 4,000.00	£ 25.00

To create a Column sparkline using VBA, you first identify the target cell where you want the sparkline to appear. Next, you call the **SparklineGroups** object's **Add** method and specify both the type of sparkline and the source of the sparkline's data. The syntax of the statement to create a Column sparkline is:

```
Range("targetrange").SparklineGroups.Add
Type:=xlSparkColumn, _
  SourceData:="source"
```

The `Type` parameter takes the value `xlSparkColumn` to signify a Column sparkline, while the `SourceData` parameter specifies the cell range supplying the sparkline's data. For example, you might create a Line sparkline in cell E1 using data from cells B4:B15.

```
Range("E1").SparklineGroups.Add
Type:=xlSparkColumn, _
    SourceData:="B4:B15"
```

⊿	A	B	C	D	E
1	**Sales for the Year**				▂▃▄▆█
2					
3	**Month**	**Sales**	**VAT**	**Target**	**Result**
4	January	£ 1,023.00	£ 250.00	£ 750.00	£ 273.00
5	February	£ 1,275.00	£ 318.75	£ 1,200.00	£ 75.00
6	March	£ 1,400.00	£ 350.00	£ 1,400.00	£ -
7	April	£ 942.00	£ 235.50	£ 1,000.00	-£ 58.00
8	May	£ 1,185.00	£ 296.25	£ 1,000.00	£ 185.00
9	June	£ 1,468.00	£ 367.00	£ 1,200.00	£ 268.00
10	July	£ 1,995.00	£ 498.75	£ 1,750.00	£ 245.00
11	August	£ 702.00	£ 175.50	£ 1,000.00	-£ 298.00
12	September	£ 1,503.00	£ 375.75	£ 1,500.00	£ 3.00
13	October	£ 1,474.00	£ 368.50	£ 1,500.00	-£ 26.00
14	November	£ 2,590.00	£ 647.50	£ 2,500.00	£ 90.00
15	December	£ 4,025.00	£ 1,006.25	£ 4,000.00	£ 25.00

Create a Column sparkline

1 Create a subroutine.

2 In the body of the subroutine, enter code that follows this pattern:

```
Range("targetrange").SparklineGroups.
Add Type:=xlSparkColumn, _
SourceData:="source"
```

For your information

Column sparklines work best in cells that are about twice the height of normal Excel cells.

10

Create a Win/
Loss sparkline

Excel provides numerous ways for you to evaluate your organisation's performance in relation to targets you set. You can use a Win/Loss sparkline to summarise your monthly sales in relation to your goals, such as in a worksheet with comparison results in cells E4:E15.

	A	B	C	D	E
1	**Sales for the Year**				
2					
3	**Month**	**Sales**	**VAT**	**Target**	**Result**
4	January	£ 1,023.00	£ 250.00	£ 750.00	£ 273.00
5	February	£ 1,275.00	£ 318.75	£ 1,200.00	£ 75.00
6	March	£ 1,400.00	£ 350.00	£ 1,400.00	£ -
7	April	£ 942.00	£ 235.50	£ 1,000.00	-£ 58.00
8	May	£ 1,185.00	£ 296.25	£ 1,000.00	£ 185.00
9	June	£ 1,468.00	£ 367.00	£ 1,200.00	£ 268.00
10	July	£ 1,995.00	£ 498.75	£ 1,750.00	£ 245.00
11	August	£ 702.00	£ 175.50	£ 1,000.00	-£ 298.00
12	September	£ 1,503.00	£ 375.75	£ 1,500.00	£ 3.00
13	October	£ 1,474.00	£ 368.50	£ 1,500.00	-£ 26.00
14	November	£ 2,590.00	£ 647.50	£ 2,500.00	£ 90.00
15	December	£ 4,025.00	£ 1,006.25	£ 4,000.00	£ 25.00

A Win/Loss sparkline has three possible indicators: above target (positive), below target (negative) and equal to the target (zero). Values above the target (also called a *comparison value*) are indicated by a marker extending above the middle of the cell, values below the target are indicated by a marker extending below the middle of the cell, while a value equal to the target is indicated by the lack of a marker.

To create a Win/Loss sparkline using VBA, you first identify the target cell where you want the sparkline to appear. Next, you call the **SparklineGroups** object's **Add** method and specify both the type of sparkline and the source of the sparkline's data. The syntax of the statement to create a Win/Loss sparkline is:

```
Range("targetrange").SparklineGroups.Add
Type:= xlSparkColumnStacked100,
SourceData:="source"
```

The `Type` parameter takes the value `xlSparkColumn Stacked100` to signify a Win/Loss sparkline, while the `SourceData` parameter specifies the cell range supplying the sparkline's data. For example, you might create a Win/Loss sparkline in cell E1 using data from cells E4:E15.

```
Range("E1").SparklineGroups.Add _
Type:= xlSparkColumnStacked100,
SourceData:="E4:E15"
```

	A	B	C	D	E
1	Sales for the Year				■ ■ ■ ■
2					
3	**Month**	**Sales**	**VAT**	**Target**	**Result**
4	January	£ 1,023.00	£ 250.00	£ 750.00	£ 273.00
5	February	£ 1,275.00	£ 318.75	£ 1,200.00	£ 75.00
6	March	£ 1,400.00	£ 350.00	£ 1,400.00	£ -
7	April	£ 942.00	£ 235.50	£ 1,000.00	-£ 58.00
8	May	£ 1,185.00	£ 296.25	£ 1,000.00	£ 185.00
9	June	£ 1,468.00	£ 367.00	£ 1,200.00	£ 268.00
10	July	£ 1,995.00	£ 498.75	£ 1,750.00	£ 245.00
11	August	£ 702.00	£ 175.50	£ 1,000.00	-£ 298.00
12	September	£ 1,503.00	£ 375.75	£ 1,500.00	£ 3.00
13	October	£ 1,474.00	£ 368.50	£ 1,500.00	-£ 26.00
14	November	£ 2,590.00	£ 647.50	£ 2,500.00	£ 90.00
15	December	£ 4,025.00	£ 1,006.25	£ 4,000.00	£ 25.00

Create a Win/Loss sparkline

1 Create a subroutine.

2 In the body of the subroutine, enter code that follows this pattern:

```
Range("targetrange").SparklineGroups.
Add _
Type:= xlSparkColumnStacked100,
SourceData:="source"
```

Did you know?

Win/Loss sparklines got their name because they are useful for tracking the performance of sports teams' wins, losses and draws.

10

Delete a sparkline

Sparklines are exceptionally useful tools, but you might find that one or more of them are surplus to your reporting requirements. In that case, you can use VBA to delete them.

The code to delete a sparkline is straightforward. The first step is to select the cell that contains the sparkline and the second is to use the **SparklineGroups** object's **Clear** method to delete them:

```
Range("cell").Select
Selection.SparklineGroups.Clear
```

The code to delete a sparkline from cell E1 would be:

```
Range("E1").Select
Selection.SparklineGroups.Clear
```

Delete a sparkline

1 Create a subroutine.

2 In the body of the subroutine, enter code that follows this pattern:

```
Range("cell").Select
Selection.SparklineGroups.Clear
```

Important

Deleting a sparkline using Excel VBA is irreversible – once you delete a sparkline, you can't bring it back by pressing Ctrl+Z.

Using built-in functions and statements

Introduction

Excel VBA is a powerful language that interacts well with the Excel desktop program. As VBA matured, its designers built in a series of capabilities that make it easier to manage exactly how that interaction takes place. For example, rather than force users to type in the full directory path of a file, you can let them select the file using the Open dialog box and save the box's output to a variable. Other built-in functions and statements let you prevent the screen from flickering when you switch between workbooks or worksheets, prevent alert boxes from interrupting your routines and calling worksheet functions so you don't have to recreate their calculations.

What you'll do

Use the built-in Open dialog box

Prevent screen flicker when running VBA code

Suppress and restore alerts

Calculate data using Excel worksheet functions

Display a message box

Get data from an InputBox

Display the current date and time

Format a date

Remove spaces from a string

Locate a portion of a string

Concatenate strings

Use the built-in Open dialog box

Most of the Excel VBA routines that new programmers create operate within the workbook that contains their code. For example, you could transfer data between worksheets, but you might not transfer the data to another workbook. As you become a more advanced Excel VBA programmer, you will likely create routines that let users specify how to proceed. For example, you might wish to allow your colleagues to select which of several files to open from within a VBA routine.

Excel 2010 lets you use the built-in Open dialog box to identify files via the user interface. The Open dialog box is the very familiar item that appears whenever you press Ctrl+O or click the File tab, then Open.

Use the built-in Open dialog box

1 Create a subroutine.

1 In the body of the subroutine, do the following:

   a. Define a variable to store the filename and path.

   b. Assign the output of the Open dialog box to the variable.

   c. Display the variable's value in a message box or use its output in your VBA code.

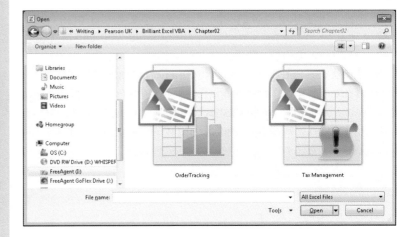

To display the Open dialog box, you use the **Application** object's **GetOpenFilename** method. Because the path and the name of your file might contain odd characters, it's best to store the value in a variable of the **Variant** type. As a simple example, you could create the following code to create a variable, assign the output of the Open dialog box to that variable, then display the value in a message box.

The code to implement those three steps is:

```
Dim varFileName as Variant
varFileName = Application.
GetOpenFilename
MsgBox ("The file's name and path are
"&varFileName)
```

Running the subroutine and selecting a file displays a message box similar to the one shown.

?

Did you know?

You could have trouble working with a file if it's stored on a network computer and the connection is down. If you have trouble finding a file, check the Network section of Windows Explorer to ensure you can see the other computer on your network.

Prevent screen flicker when running VBA code

Prevent screen flicker when running VBA code

1 Create a subroutine.

2 In the body of the subroutine, enter code that follows this pattern:

```
Application.
ScreenUpdating =
True or False
```

Whenever you activate a worksheet or a workbook using Excel VBA, the program displays that worksheet or workbook. Usually this means the program has to switch from whichever element is displayed on screen to a new element. A single switch between two worksheets or workbooks doesn't create much of problem, but if you create complicated routines that switch back and forth several times, the screen can appear to flicker.

Even though this flickering doesn't slow the execution of your code, it can be very distracting, especially if you have created a long-running routine and you want to do other work. You can prevent screen flicker by turning off screen updating using the **Application.ScreenUpdating** property. When the property is set to **False**, the screen will not update to reflect any changes made to the active worksheet or workbook, or to indicate that the program focus has changed to another worksheet or workbook.

The Excel VBA command used to prevent screen flicker is:

```
Application.ScreenUpdating = False
```

When your code is done switching between worksheets or workbooks and you want to display the results, you can turn screen updating back on by using this code:

```
Application.ScreenUpdating = True
```

For your information

Even though Excel turns screen updating back on when it completes running a VBA routine, it's good practice to include the **Application.ScreenUpdating = True** command in your code just in case you need to interact with the program before it's finished executing.

Many operations, such as deleting a worksheet, cause Excel to display an alert box indicating that the action you are about to take is irreversible or could have some other, possibly harmful effect. These warnings are helpful in that they prevent users from inadvertently removing important parts of the workbook, but they prevent the smooth operation of the VBA routines that generate those messages.

For example, suppose you create a VBA routine that includes instructions to delete a worksheet. When you run the routine, Excel will reach that line of code and attempt to delete the worksheet but, rather than just deleting the worksheet, the program will display the alert box asking if you're certain that you want to go ahead with the deletion. Getting past the alert box requires human intervention, which can prevent the full execution of your program.

If you are certain that the action you program into a VBA routine should be executed regardless of these warnings, you can suppress alerts. The code to do so is:

```
Application.DisplayAlerts = False
```

After your code has executed the instructions that could generate an alert, you should turn alert and warning messages back on. Doing so lets you avoid damaging your workbook by having your VBA code make an unintended change you can't reverse.

The statement to have Excel display alert and warning boxes again is:

```
Application.ScreenUpdating = True
```

Suppress and restore alerts

1 Create a subroutine.

2 In the body of the subroutine, enter code that follows this pattern:

```
Application.
ScreenUpdating =
True or False
```

Important

You should not turn off alerts while you are testing a program. Only after you are certain that your VBA code operates exactly as you expect should you suppress alerts.

Calculate data using Excel worksheet functions

Calculate data using Excel worksheet functions

 Create a subroutine.

 In the body of the subroutine, enter code that follows this pattern:

```
Application.
WorksheetFunction.
function(arguments)
```

Microsoft Excel 2010 is an exceptionally powerful and versatile program, with many built-in functions you can use to transform data into useful information. You are not limited to using those formula functions in a worksheet. Rather than create your own calculations and risk introducing errors into the process, you can call on a wide array of worksheet functions from within VBA.

To use a worksheet function in your VBA code, you start by typing this fragment of VBA code:

```
Application.WorksheetFunction.
```

The final full stop in the above fragment indicates you need to add another element to the statement to make it functional. In this case, that element is the name of the function you want to use. There are hundreds of functions at your disposal, which appear in the AutoComplete list when you type the code fragment above.

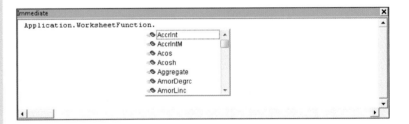

You can select the function you want by typing in its name, selecting it from the AutoComplete list or a combination of both actions. After you add the function name to the code fragment and type a left parenthesis, the Visual Basic Editor displays a list of arguments you can use in the formula. Required arguments are listed in bold italic type, optional arguments in normal italic type.

You can then supply values for the arguments by typing their values, such as cell ranges, directly into the Visual Basic Editor or by using values assigned to variables.

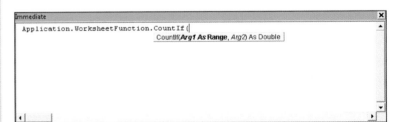

When you create or edit an Excel worksheet via the user interface, you get immediate feedback on what you've done because the worksheet changes. Most users will take a moment to survey what they have done to ensure their actions had the intended outcome. When you run a VBA routine, you don't have that luxury. The speed of execution prevents any meaningful feedback from a user before the code finishes running.

One a terrific way to provide user feedback as part of a VBA routine is to display the result of an action or information about an action using a message box. As the name implies, a message box is a dialog box that displays information of your choosing. You can set the message box's title, message and the buttons that appear within it. A simple message box might look like this:

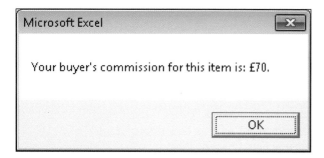

Message boxes have many attributes that you can control using VBA, but the first three are the most useful. The syntax to display a message box using those three arguments is:

```
MsgBox(prompt, buttons, title)
```

where:

- **prompt** is the text that appears in the body of the message box (required)

- **buttons** are clickable buttons, such as 'OK' or 'Cancel', that appear in the body of the message box (optional)

- **title** is the text that appears on the message box's title bar (optional).

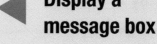

Display a message box

1 Create a subroutine.

2 In the body of the subroutine, enter code that follows one of these patterns:

```
MsgBox(prompt)
MsgBox
Prompt:=string,
Buttons:=constant,
Title:=string
```

Display a message box (cont.)

The prompt argument usually takes the form of a string assigned to a variable. You can create a simple message box by typing the string into the command, such as:

```
MsgBox("Click OK to continue.")
```

That said, many times you will want to combine several values in the message. For example, you might have a routine that calculates sales commissions. If the sales amount were in the active cell, you could assign the first part of the prompt to one variable and then add the value to the string using the '&' concatenation operator.

```
Sub CalculateCommission()
Dim curSale As Currency
Dim curCommission As Currency
Dim strPrompt1 As String
Dim strPromptAll As String

curSale = ActiveCell.Value
curCommission = curSale * 0.15
strPrompt1 = "The commission due for
this sale is: £"
strPromptAll = strPrompt1 &
curCommission & "."

MsgBox (strPromptAll)
End Sub
```

You can also control which buttons appear in your message box. If you leave the argument blank, the message box will contain an 'OK' button the user can click to dismiss the message box. Table 11.1 shows the other button patterns available to you and the values to which they correspond.

Table 11.1 Constants used to specify message box buttons

Constant	Value	Description
vbOKOnly	0	Display the 'OK' button only
vbOKCancel	1	Display the 'OK' and 'Cancel' buttons
vbAbortRetry Ignore	2	Display the 'Abort', 'Retry', and 'Ignore' buttons
vbYesNoCancel	3	Display the 'Yes', 'No', and 'Cancel' buttons
vbYesNo	4	Display the 'Yes' and 'No' buttons
vbRetryCancel	5	Display the 'Retry' and 'Cancel' buttons

When a user clicks a button in a message box, their action returns a value you can use to affect your code. For example, a manager might get to decide whether a transaction earns a bonus in addition to the usual commission. The button values are shown in Table 11.2.

Table 11.2 Return values of message box buttons

Constant	Value	Description
vbOK	1	OK
vbCancel	2	Cancel
vbAbort	3	Abort
vbRetry	4	Retry
vbIgnore	5	Ignore
vbYes	6	Yes
vbNo	7	No

The code to create a message box with 'Yes' and 'No' buttons and then to calculate commission plus bonus (if any) due on a sale would be:

```
Sub CommissionPlusBonus()
Dim curSale As Currency
```

Display a message box (cont.)

```
Dim curCommission As Currency
Dim curBonus as Currency
Dim strPrompt1 As String
Dim strPromptAll As String
Dim intBonus as Integer

curSale = ActiveCell.Value
intBonus = MsgBox("Bonus due?", vbYesNo)
If intBonus = 6 Then
    curCommission = curSale * 0.2
  Else: curCommission = curSale * 0.15
End IfstrPrompt1 = "The commission due
for this sale is: £"
strPromptAll = strPrompt1 &
curCommission & "."

MsgBox (strPromptAll)
End Sub
```

See also

For more information on **If...Then...ElseIf** statements, see Chapter 12.

Finally, you can set the title to appear on the message box's title bar. That value won't usually change, but you could still assign its value to a variable to make the **MsgBox** statement shorter. You should also use parameters, rather than arguments, to specify the **MsgBox** statement's attributes. As an example, you could use the following statement:

```
MsgBox Prompt:=strPromptAll,
Buttons:=vbYesNo, Title:="Commission"
```

Running the previous code would generate a message box with the title 'Commission', 'Yes' and 'No' buttons and a prompt that reflects the value of variable **strPromptAll**.

Did you know?

To create a message box with just an 'OK' button, set the buttons argument to '0' or leave it blank.

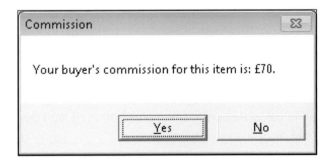

One of the difficulties of programming in Excel VBA is incorporating user input into a routine that is underway. If you create a worksheet that contains several cells clearly marked as requiring user input, you can have the user enter their information into worksheet cells and then run your code. Alternatively, if your code is currently running, you will either need to direct the user to enter data into specific cells and then click another button before proceeding or capture that same data using an InputBox.

Like a message box, discussed in the previous section, an InputBox displays a message you specify. The difference is that there are controls within the box that can accept user input, such as typed words or a cell range the user selects from the active worksheet.

The **Application.InputBox** method can take several parameters, but the three you will use most often are:

1 **Prompt** the text to display within the InputBox (required)

2 **Title** the text that appears on the title bar of the InputBox (optional)

3 **Type** the type of InputBox to display (optional – InputBox types are summarised in Table 11.3).

Table 11.3 Values for the InputBox method's Type parameter

Value	Meaning
0	A formula
1	A number
2	Text (a string)
4	A logical value ('True' or 'False')
8	A cell reference, as a Range object
16	An error value, such as #N/A
64	An array of values

Get data from an InputBox (cont.)

As an example, suppose you require information about a percentage discount to be applied it to a customer's order. You can gather that information using an InputBox and assign it to a variable, as in the following code:

```
curOffer = Application.InputBox("Please
enter your offer for the item.")
```

If you wanted to add a title to the InputBox, you could do so as follows:

```
curOffer = Application.InputBox (Prompt:=
"Enter an offer", Title:= "Offer")
```

The two code examples shown earlier assume you want a value such as a number or text string. If you want the user to identify a range of cells using the InputBox, you need to assign the proper value to the **Type** parameter. As shown in Table 11.3, setting the **Type** parameter to 8 lets the user select a range of cells. That code might look like this:

```
Dim rngValueRange as Range
Set rngValueRange = Application.
InputBox("Select a range.", Type:=8)
MsgBox(rngValueRange.Address)
```

Running this code displays an InputBox that accepts a selected range as its input.

Get data from an InputBox

1 Create a subroutine.

2 In the body of the subroutine, enter code that follows this pattern:

```
curOffer =
Application.
InputBox
(Prompt:string,
Title:=string,
Type:=number)
```

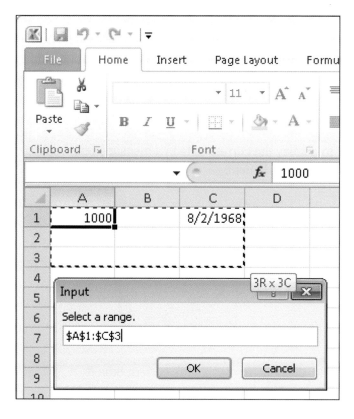

Did you know?

The values you can assign to the **Type** parameter are additive, meaning that if you want to allow a number (1) or a text string (2), you can add them together to create an assignment statement such as **Type:=3**.

Important

If you set the **Type** parameter to 64, you must define the variable to which you assign the InputBox's value as an array.

Display the current date and time

Display the current date and time

1. Create a subroutine.

2. In the body of the subroutine, enter code that follows one of these patterns:

```
Date()
Time()
```

Did you know?

The specific format displayed by the date and time functions depends on your computer's regional settings.

Any data you gather could provide valuable information about your organisation's performance, but you need to ensure you know when the information was gathered. Updating a database daily with last year's information is not a sound business practice.

To display the current date, use the statement **Date()**. If you want to display the current date in a message box, you can use the following statement:

```
MsgBox(Date())
```

Similarly, the code to display the current time is:

```
MsgBox(Time())
```

You can treat the date and time values as strings and combine them into a single message box using the code:

```
MsgBox(Date & " " & Time())
```

Dates are important, regardless of whether they refer to the start of a project, the anniversary of an event or the completion date of a future project. It's absolutely vital that you communicate dates clearly, whether in your worksheet or any your Excel VBA programs. The format you select for your dates depends on your audience and industry standards, but you can display dates in several formats using Excel VBA.

To display a date or time value in a specific format, use the **FormatDateTime** method, which has the following syntax:

```
FormatDateTime(Cells(row, column),
format)
```

You must use the **Cells** property, not the **Range** property, to identify the cell that contains the date you want to display. Note that the row comes first, followed by the column. You must refer to the column by number, not letter. For example, you refer to cell C1 (row 1, column 3) as:

```
Cells(1, 3)
```

The **Format** argument can take on one of five values, as shown in Table 11.4.

Table 11.4 Constants used to specify date and time formats

Constant	Description
vbGeneral Date	Display a date and/or time. If there is a date part, display it as a short date. If there is a time part, display it as a long time. If present, both parts are displayed
vbLong Date	Display a date using the long date format specified in your computer's regional settings
vbShort Date	Display a date using the short date format specified in your computer's regional settings
vbLong Time	Display a time using the time format specified in your computer's regional settings
vbShort Time	Display a time using the 24-hour format (hh:mm)

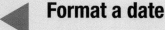

Format a date

Format a date

1 Create a subroutine.

2 In the body of the subroutine, enter code that follows this pattern:

```
FormatDateTime
(Cells(row, column),
format)
```

11

Format a date (cont.)

If cell C1 contains a time, you can assign that time, written in the 24-hour format, to a string variable using this statement:

```
strTimeValue =
FormatDateTime(Cells(1,3), vbShortTime)
```

To display the time, create a message box that uses the **strTimeValue** variable as its prompt:

```
MsgBox(strTimeValue)
```

Did you know?

You can determine the number of a column by remembering the mnemonic EJOTY. E is the fifth letter of the alphabet, J is the tenth, O the fifteenth, T the twentieth and Y the twenty-fifth. Just find a letter close to the column's letter and count up or down as required.

Excel 2010 is ideally suited to handling numbers, but it is also extremely effective at managing textual data. Whether your worksheets contain information such as product names or descriptions, customer names and addresses or salutations to be used as part of a mail merge program, you will find surprising amounts of text in your worksheets.

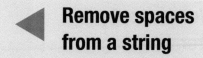
To get the best results from Excel's text-handling capabilities, you should ensure that the text strings in your workbook contain as few errors as possible. One of the most common errors is for Excel string data to have excess spaces, whether entered by people pressing the spacebar when they shouldn't or by transferring a file from another database format that happens to include blank spaces with the data so that every field contains values of the same length.

You can use three different VBA functions to remove spaces from a string: `Trim`, `LTrim` and `RTrim`.

1 `Trim` removes excess blank spaces from the beginning and end of a string

2 `LTrim` removes excess blank spaces from the beginning (that is, the left end) of a string

3 `RTrim` removes excess blank spaces from the end (that is, the right end) of a string.

The syntax of each function is quite straightforward and follows this pattern:

```
Trim(string)
```

You can also use a cell reference, such as:

```
Trim(Range("cell"))
```

If the string is assigned to a variable, you can use the variable's name in place of the string or cell reference. If you specify the string, you must enclose it within double quotes:

```
Trim("    commission due.    ")
```

Remove spaces from a string (cont.)

Remove spaces from a string

1 Create a subroutine.

2 In the body of the subroutine, enter code that follows this pattern:

```
Trim$(string)
```

One peculiarity of the **Trim**, **LTrim** and **RTrim** functions is that they return a result of type **Variant**, rather than type **String**. If you want to force these functions to return a string, you can add a dollar sign ($) to the end of the function name. Combining this code with a message box statement, such as:

```
MsgBox(Trim$("      Thank you for your
order.     "))
```

would return the following result shown in the figure.

Did you know?

None of the functions removes excess spaces from the *interior* of a string. If there are multiple spaces within a string's text, these functions assume they are supposed to be there.

Text strings, such as product names or stockkeeping units (SKUs), often have quite a bit of information built into them. For example, a vehicle identification number might contain information about the make, year and model of that vehicle. If you want to extract a specific part of that information from the string, you can do so using VBA, as long as the data follows an identifiable pattern.

You can use three functions to return portions of a text string: **Left**, **Right** and **Mid**. The **Left** and **Right** functions return a given number of characters from a string, starting from either the left or right end. The basic syntax of the **Left** function is:

```
Left(string, length)
```

The syntax for **Right** is exactly the same, except it counts from the *right* end of the string. As an example, suppose you have a value CA042908BU assigned to the variable **strProductID**. If the first two characters represent the product's department, you can display them using this code:

```
MsgBox(Left(strProductID, 2))
```

Similarly, if the last four characters of the **ProductID** (those at the right end of the string) represent the model and colour of the product, you could assign them to a variable using this code:

```
MsgBox(Right(strProductID, 4))
```

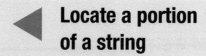
Locate a portion of a string

1 Create a subroutine.

2 In the body of the subroutine, enter code that follows this pattern:

```
Left(string, length)
Right(strProductID,4)
Mid(strProductID,7,2)
```

Locate a portion of a string (cont.)

You can find a value from the middle of a string using the **Mid** function, the syntax for which is different from, but similar to, that for **Left** and **Right**:

```
Mid(string, start, count)
```

where:

- **string** is the string (a literal string, a variable or a range reference)

- **start** is the character at which to start returning the value

- **count** is the number of characters to return, including the first.

For example, if the value of **strProductID** were CA042908BU, the following code would display the seventh and eighth characters – 08:

```
MsgBox(Mid(strProductID, 7, 2))
```

The **Left**, **Right** and **Mid** functions return **Variant** values by default. If you want to force them to return strings, add a dollar sign ($) to the end of the function name (such as, **Left$**).

Many of the actions you will take in Excel workbook involve data from several different sources. For example, a customer order could contain information such as the customer's first name, last name and address, as well as the order amount and any tax or postage due. If you want to create a confirmation message, such as by using a message box, you will need to combine those a several bits of information into a single string to be displayed in the message box.

Combining bits of text into a single string is called *concatenation*. Concatenation is handled in Excel VBA by using the ampersand character (&). For example, you could assign text to a string variable, a currency value to another variable and combine those variables with other values into a single message box prompt. For example:

```
Dim strPrompt1 as String
Dim strPromptAll as String
Dim curBuyerCom as Currency
curBuyerCom = ActiveCell.Value * 0.07
strPrompt1 = "Your buyer's commission
for this item is: £"
strPromptAll = strPrompt1 & curBuyerCom
& "."
MsgBox (strPromptAll)
```

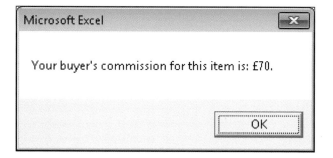

Concatenate strings

1 Create a subroutine.

2 In the body of the subroutine, enter code that follows this pattern:

```
strFullString
= strString1 &
strString2 & …
```

?

Did you know?

You can also use the '&' character to concatenate values in worksheet formulas, such as =C2 & C3.

Managing code using logical constructs

Introduction

Many Excel VBA routines are straightforward – when you run them from the Macros dialog box or by clicking a worksheet object, they execute their code and the result appears in your workbook. As your workbooks become more complex, you will no doubt find that you must decide when a macro should run and, in some cases, which of several paths it should take. In this chapter, you will learn how to control your VBA code using logical constructs such as the **For**...**Next** and **For**...**Each** loops, **If**...**Then** statements, **Case** statements and other techniques.

Create a For... Next loop

Much of the code you write in Excel VBA will be executed once in a subroutine. For example, you could display a message box with the name of a customer, find the date a delivery is due or look up the wholesale price of an item from a distributor. If you do need to repeat a segment of your code, perhaps looking up multiple prices or customer names, you can do so using a **For**...**Next** loop:

```
For counter = start To finish
Code
Next counter
```

The loop structure begins at the **start** value, executes the code in the body of the loop, increases the counter value by one, then returns to the **For** statement, where the counter value increases. The process repeats until the counter exceeds the finish value.

For example, you might have a series of five prices in cells A2:A6. If you want to read those values into a VBA array, you could do so using this code:

```
Dim curPrices(4) as Currency
Dim intCounter as Integer
Range("A2").Activate
For intCounter = 0 To 4
curPrices(intCounter) = ActiveCell.
Offset(intCounter, 0).Value
Next intCounter
```

By default, each step in a **For**...**Next** loop increases the counter value by one. You can move through a **For**...**Next** loop in different increments by specifying a **Step** value. For example, you could display every other element in an array by using a **Step** value of two:

```
For intCounter = 0 To 4 Step 2
MsgBox(curPrices(intCounter))
Next intCounter
```

If you'd like to work backwards through an array, you can make the start value larger than the finish value and specify a *negative* **Step** increment:

```
For intCounter = 4 To 0 Step -1
MsgBox(curPrices(intCounter))
Next intCounter
```

Create a **For**...**Next** loop

1 Create a subroutine.

2 In the body of the subroutine.

   a. create a For...Next loop

   b. create a For...Next loop with a **Step** parameter.

Did you know?

If you have trouble moving through every element in an array using a **For**...**Next** loop, remember that arrays are numbered from zero in Excel VBA.

For...**Next** loops are useful, straightforward code constructs that let you repeat your code a set number of times. The difficulty arises when you don't know (or don't want to take the time to discover) how many times you want to repeat the code.

As an example, suppose you want to add the string '*2012*' to every sheet name in a workbook. It's certainly possible to use the **Sheets** collection's **Count** property to discover the number of sheets in a workbook, but you then have to assign that value to the **For**...**Next** loop's counter variable. Fortunately, there is a way to step through a collection of objects without using a counter. That technique is the **For**...**Each** loop.

The basic structure of the **For**...**Each** loop is as follows:

```
For Each element In collection
  Code
Next element
```

As a simple example, suppose you have an array named **curPrices** and want to display each value in a message box. Rather than count the number of elements in the array and use that result in a **For**...**Next** loop, you can use a **For**...**Each** loop to display each value:

```
Dim var as Variant
For Each var in Collection
MsgBox(var)
Next var
```

When you use a **For**...**Each** loop to refer to objects, such as workbooks or worksheets, you must define object variables to represent them in the loop. To return to our example, to use VBA code to add the string '*2012*' to the end of every worksheet's name in the active workbook, you could use this subroutine:

```
Sub WorksheetNames()
Dim wbk As Workbook
Dim wks As Worksheet

Set wbk = ThisWorkbook
For Each wks In wbk.Worksheets
    wks.Name = wks.Name & "2012"
Next wks
Set wbk = Nothing
End Sub
```

Create a For... Each loop

Create a For...Each loop

1. Create a subroutine.

2. In the body of the subroutine, enter code that follows this pattern:

```
Dim var as Variant
For Each var in
Collection
  <action>
Next var
```

12

Did you know?

Using a variable of type **Variant** as your **For**...**Each** loop counter lets you refer to any type of data, including objects such as workbooks or worksheets.

Create an If...
Then statement

Create an If...Then... ElseIf statement:

1. Create a subroutine.

2. In the body of the subroutine, enter code that follows one of these patterns:

   a. If...Then on a single line.

   b. If...Then...Else, where Else appears on its own line.

   c. If...Then...ElseIf... Else, where ElseIf and Else appear on their own lines.

Life is rarely simple, especially when your affairs have progressed to the point where you require VBA to customise the workbooks you use to track them. If the procedure you want your workbook to follow varies according to the data it contains, you can use If...Then statements to determine which path to follow.

Excel VBA includes several types of If...Then statements. The first variation is the IIf function, which is an implementation of the workbook function IF. The syntax for the IIf function is exactly the same as that of the workbook function:

```
IIf(test, value_if_true, value_if_false)
```

As an example, you might want to grant 6 per cent commission for any sale greater than £500 and 4 per cent otherwise. To calculate that commission based on the value in the active cell, you could create a subroutine using the IIf function:

```
Sub CalculateCommission()
Dim curSaleValue as Currency
Dim curCommission as Currency
curSaleValue = ActiveCell.Value
curCommission = IIf(curSaleValue>
500,curSaleValue * 0.06, _
  curSaleValue * 0.04)
MsgBox ("£" & curCommission)
End Sub
```

The best time to use the IIf function is when you have a working IF formula in a worksheet and want to copy it over directly – with the caveat that any cell references from the formula must be updated so they work in VBA. That said, complex or nested IF formulas can be hard for humans to read. If you have a complex IF formula or if you want to create a new conditional statement in VBA, it's much easier to use the If...Then construction.

The basic form of the `If`...`Then` construct asks if a condition is true. If it is, the routine runs the code within the construct; otherwise, it does nothing.

```
If test Then action
```

For example, you could examine the value of a sale and, if it exceeds a threshold level, display a message indicating that the sale qualifies for a bonus.

```
Sub OneLineIfThen()
If ActiveCell.Value >= 1000 Then MsgBox
("Sale qualifies for bonus.")
End Sub
```

If you require a bit more flexibility, such as executing separate sets of instructions based on whether the condition is true or not, you can use an `If`...`Then`...`Else` statement to manage your program's logic:

```
If test Then
  Code if the condition is true
  Else
    Code if the condition is false
End If

Sub OneElse()
Dim curCommission as Currency
If ActiveCell.Value >= 1000 Then
    curCommission = ActiveCell.Value *
    0.06
    Else
        curCommission = ActiveCell.Value
        * 0.05
End If

MsgBox ("£" & curCommission)
End Sub
```

In the same way that you can manage true or false conditions using an `If`...`Then`...`Else` construction, you can manage three or more conditions using an `If`...`ElseIf` construction. The `ElseIf` keyword, which can be repeated, lets you establish multiple conditions:

Important

Note that the `Else` keyword appears on its own line in the code listing. If it doesn't, the VBA interpreter will flag it as an error.

Create an `If`... `Then` statement (cont.)

```
If condition1 Then
Code1
ElseIf condition2 Then
Code2
ElseIf condition3 Then
Code3

Else
Code
End If
```

The canonical example for **`If`**...**`ElseIf`** constructions is that of calculating sales commissions based on sales amounts. For instance, you could set differing commission rates for sales of the £10,000, £5,000, £1,000 and below £1,000 levels.

```
Sub ElseIfExample()
Dim curCommission as Currency

If ActiveCell.Value >= 10000 Then
    curCommission = ActiveCell.Value *
0.08
    ElseIf ActiveCell.Value >= 5000 Then
            curCommission = ActiveCell.
Value * 0.07
    ElseIf ActiveCell.Value >= 1000 Then
        curCommission = ActiveCell.Value
* 0.06
    Else
    curCommission = ActiveCell.Value *
0.05
End If

MsgBox ("£" & curCommission)
End Sub
```

Note that the **`ElseIf`**...**`Then`** lines are constructed in exactly the same manner as **`If`**...**`Then`** lines. Also, as with **`If`**...**`Then`**...**`Else`** statements, the **`Else`** keyword must appear on its own line.

Excel VBA offers two main ways to conditionally execute code: `If`...`Then` constructions and `Case` constructions. The two constructions have similar effects on your code, so which one you use is largely a matter of taste. Some programmers find that the `Case Is` syntax is easier to read for more than two or three conditions, so they tend to use them when their code must distinguish four or more cases.

The `Case` statement has the following general syntax:

```
Select Case variable
Case Is condition1
Action1
Case Is condition2
Action2

Case Else
Action else
End Select
```

You may have as many `Case Is` statements as you like but only one `Case Else` statement, which must also be the last statement in the `Select Case` structure. Code to calculate sales commissions using a `Case` statement could take on the following form:

```
Sub SelectRate()

Dim curTotal As Currency
curTotal = ActiveCell.Value

Select Case curTotal
Case Is >= 10000
    curCommission = curTotal * 0.08
Case Is >= 1000
    curCommission = curTotal * 0.06
Case Is >= 500
    curCommission = curTotal * 0.05
Case Else
    curCommission = curTotal * 0.04
End Select

MsgBox ("Your commission is £" &
curCommission)
End Sub
```

Create a `Case` statement

Create a `Case` statement

1 Create a subroutine.

2 In the body of the subroutine, enter code that follows this pattern:

```
Select Case
Case Is condition
```
  (this line is repeatable for different conditions)
```
Case Else
```

12

Important

If the comparison value doesn't fit any of the `Case Is` criteria, the `Select Case` statement returns a value of zero.

Did you know?

As with `If`...`Then` statements, Excel VBA stops checking `Case` statement as soon as it encounters a true condition.

Create a Do loop

Create a Do loop

1. Create a subroutine.

2. In the body of the subroutine, enter code that follows this pattern:

```
Do

    Code

    Test Then Exit Do

    Code

Loop
```

For...Next and For...Each constructions, described earlier in this chapter, let you repeat code as long as a counter variable stays within a given range or until every member of a collection has been touched by the code. If your conditions are more variable, such as when you're examining inventory or loading a truck up to but not over a known capacity, you can use a Do loop.

A Do loop repeats a section of code until it encounters the Exit Do statement, which causes the program to jump out of the loop and execute the next instruction below the Loop statement in the code module.

The Do loop has the following general syntax:

```
Do
    Code
    Test Then Exit Do
    Code
Loop
```

Programmers can use an If...Then or other conditional statement to determine if the condition to exit the loop has been met. For example, you could create a Do loop that locates the first blank cell in column B of the worksheet named 'Orders'.

```
Sub FindFirstEmptyDL()
Worksheets("Orders").Activate
Range("B1").Activate
Do
    If ActiveCell.Value = "" Then Exit Do
    ActiveCell.Offset(1, 0).Activate
Loop
End Sub
```

See also

For more information on If...Then and other conditional statements, see elsewhere in this chapter.

Important

Be sure to test your code to ensure the condition you set can be met. If it can't, your code will run indefinitely until you press Ctrl+C to end it.

212

The basic **Do** loop uses an internal construction, such as an **If**...**Then** statement, to determine when to exit the loop by invoking an **Exit Do** statement. That construction is easy to understand, but it's not as compact as it might be. One alternative is to use a **Do**...**While** loop, which executes the code within the loop once and checks whether or not a condition is still **True**. If the condition is met, Excel executes the code within the loop and repeats its check, either returning to the top of the loop or continuing with the next line in the subroutine.

The **Do**...**While** loop has the following basic syntax:

```
Do
   Code
Loop While condition
```

For example, you could find the total weight of packages to be loaded on to a truck and keep adding to the list while the total weight is less than or equal to 1000 kg.

```
Sub LoadWeight()
Dim sngTotalWeight as Single
Worksheets("Loading").Activate
Range("A2").Activate
sngTotalWeight = 0

Do
    sngTotalWeight = sngTotalWeight +
    ActiveCell.Value
    ActiveCell.Offset(1, 0).Activate
Loop While sngTotalWeight + ActiveCell.
Value <= 1000
MsgBox ("Total weight is " &
sngTotalWeight & " kg.")
End Sub
```

Microsoft Excel

Total weight is 600 kg.

OK

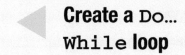

Create a Do... While loop

Create a Do...While loop

1. Create a subroutine.

2. In the body of the subroutine, enter code that follows this pattern:

```
Do

   Code

Loop While condition
```

12

Did you know?

You could add an **If**...**Then** statement inside the **Do**...**While** loop to alert you if a package has a listed weight of more than 1000 kg.

Create a Do... Until loop

Loops that follow the `Do...While` pattern execute a block of code once before checking whether or not a condition is still True. If it is, the loop repeats, checks again and either exits the loop or goes back to the top. The `Do...Until` loop is similar, but it phrases the condition differently. If the condition, such as a minimum value of items in a gift pack, has not been met, the loop repeats. If it has, Excel steps out of the loop and executes the next instruction in the subroutine.

Create a Do...Until loop

1. Create a subroutine.

2. In the body of the subroutine, enter code that follows this pattern:

```
Do

    Code

Loop Until
condition
```

The `Do...Until` loop has the following general syntax:

```
Do
   Code
Loop Until condition
```

To return the example mentioned earlier, you could create a routine that adds items to a gift basket until a minimum value has been reached. The loop would track the value of each item and exit when the minimum was reached.

```
Sub MakeBasket()
Dim curTotalValue as Currency
Worksheets("Items").Activate
Range("A2").Activate
curTotalValue = 0

Do
    curTotalValue = curTotalValue +
    ActiveCell.Value
    ActiveCell.Offset(1, 0).Activate
Loop Until curTotalValue >= 50
MsgBox ("Total value is £" &
curTotalValue & ".")
End Sub
```

Did you know?

The `Do...While` and `Do...Until` loops can have equivalent behaviours, so use the construction that best fits how you want to phrase the condition that controls their function.

214

One terrific feature of object-oriented programming is the ability to write your code in a modular fashion. What modular means in this context is that you can create a small, discrete unit of code to which you can refer from other blocks of code instead of recreating it every time you need its functionality.

For example, suppose you create a subroutine to display a message box that contains the commission due for a sale.

```
Sub CalculateCommission(curTotal as
Currency)

Select Case curTotal
Case Is >= 10000
    curCommission = curTotal * 0.08
Case Is >= 1000
    curCommission = curTotal * 0.06
Case Is >= 500
    curCommission = curTotal * 0.05
Case Else
    curCommission = curTotal * 0.04
End Select

MsgBox ("Your commission is £" &
curCommission)
End Sub
```

Rather than write and rewrite this somewhat lengthy **Case** statement whenever you need to calculate a commission, you can call it from another routine by name. The following subroutine takes the value from the active cell, displays it as the sales amount, and then calls the **CalculateCommission** subroutine listed above to display the commission due:

```
Sub DisplaySale()
Dim curSale As Currency

curSale = ActiveCell.Value
MsgBox ("Sale value is £" & curSale)
CalculateCommission (curSale)

End Sub
```

Call another macro from within your code

Call another macro from within your code

12

1 Create a subroutine.

2 In the body of the subroutine, enter code that follows this pattern:

RoutineName (arguments)

Did you know?

In older versions of Excel VBA, you had to use the **Call** keyword to execute another macro.

Refer to objects using a `With...End With` statement

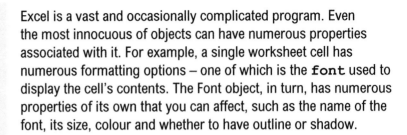

Refer to objects using a `With...End With` statement

1 Create a subroutine.

2 In the body of the subroutine, enter code that follows this pattern:

```
With object
  .Property1
  .Property2...
End With
```

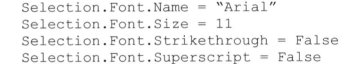
Did you know?

Recording a macro that affects the workbook object you want to control often produces a `With...End With` construct you can use as a template for your code.

Excel is a vast and occasionally complicated program. Even the most innocuous of objects can have numerous properties associated with it. For example, a single worksheet cell has numerous formatting options – one of which is the **font** used to display the cell's contents. The Font object, in turn, has numerous properties of its own that you can affect, such as the name of the font, its size, colour and whether to have outline or shadow.

To apply a series of formatting options using standard notation, you would use a series of statements such as:

```
Selection.Font.Name = "Arial"
Selection.Font.Size = 11
Selection.Font.Strikethrough = False
Selection.Font.Superscript = False
```

Typing the **`Selection.Font`** leader for each line is time-consuming and, thankfully, unnecessary due to the **`With...End With`** construction:

```
With object.property
.property1 = value
.property2 = value

End With
```

For example, if you wanted to format a cell's text, you could do so using the following code:

```
Sub FormatCell()
    Range("A2").Select
    With Selection.Font
        .Name = "Arial"
        .Size = 11
        .Strikethrough = False
        .Superscript = False
        .Subscript = False
        .OutlineFont = False
        .Shadow = False
        .Underline = xlUnderlineStyleNone
        .ThemeColor = xlThemeColorLight1
        .TintAndShade = 0
        .ThemeFont = xlThemeFontNone
    End With
End Sub
```

Debugging your VBA code

Introduction

Writing VBA code is a tricky business. VBA is a well-defined language, but it's easy for human beings to make mistakes, whether in code syntax, logic or the occasional spelling error. Here, you'll learn various techniques to track your variables throughout a subroutine's execution, examine your code's behaviour step by step and handle errors that occur.

Execute code in the Immediate window

Execute code in the Immediate window

1. If necessary, in the Visual Basic Editor, click View, then Immediate Window to display the Immediate Window.

2. Type the line of code you want to execute and then press Enter.

Several of the techniques you will learn in this chapter involve stepping through a VBA procedure one instruction at a time. If you are moving through a VBA procedure in this way, you might want to check on the value of a variable or the address of the active cell as you go. You can certainly create a **MsgBox** statement to display the value of a variable at a given point, but you will either have to add a message box every time you want the value to be displayed or edit your code to change the position of the statement.

Rather than add an instruction to your subroutine, you can type it in the Immediate window. The Immediate window appears at the bottom of the Visual Basic Editor; if it doesn't appear, you can display it by clicking View, then Immediate Window in the menu.

To use the Immediate window, type a single line of code in the window, then press Enter. When you do, Excel executes that code and displays the result. For example, you could type the command **MsgBox (ActiveCell.Address)** in the Immediate window. When you press Enter, the Visual Basic Editor will display a message box that contains the address of the active cell in the immediate window.

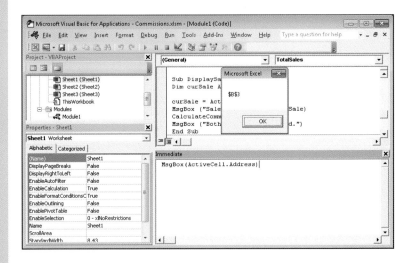

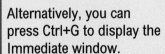

Did you know?

Alternatively, you can press Ctrl+G to display the Immediate window.

When you test a VBA routine, you might want to stop your code executing without exiting the subroutine entirely. You could display a message box containing a value of interest, which is a very common and extremely useful technique, but you could also define a breakpoint in your VBA code so you can investigate the values assigned to any of your variables without creating a message box for each one.

To add a breakpoint your code, display the module that contains your subroutine then, in the vertical bar at the left side of the code window, click next to the line where you want to pause. Doing so displays a brick red circle in the bar and highlights the line in your subroutine to indicate where your code will stop executing.

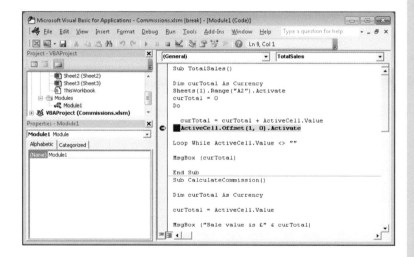

While your code is stopped, you can hover your mouse pointer over any variable in your code to display a tool tip that contains the variable assigned to the value.

When you've finished investigating your code, pressing the F5 key resumes the execution of the code. You can remove the breakpoint by clicking its circle in the vertical bar.

Set a breakpoint in your VBA code

Set a breakpoint in your VBA code

1 In the vertical bar that runs along the left edge of the code window, click to display a brick red circle that represents the breakpoint.

2 Click a breakpoint circle to remove it from the Visual Basic Editor.

13

Did you know?

To halt your code's execution instead of completing the run, click **Run...Break** on the menu bar or press Ctrl+Break.

Important

If your breakpoint occurs inside a loop, it's possible your code will stop more than once.

Watch a value in a routine

When you create a complicated subroutine, it will often be difficult for you to follow the values of specific variables as they change during the code's execution. You can use breakpoints to halt your code and display the values you're interested in. What's more, breakpoints are particularly effective in combination with watches.

In the Visual Basic Editor, a *watch* displays the value of variables you identify. To create a watch, click **Debug**... **Add Watch** on the menu bar. When you do, the Add Watch dialog box appears.

Watch a value in a routine

1. Click **Debug...Add Watch**.
2. Type the name of the variable you want to monitor in the Expression box.
3. Click OK.
4. To manage a watch, do one the following:
   a. Right-click the watch and click Edit Watch to display the Edit Watch dialog box.
   b. Right-click the watch and click Delete Watch to delete it.

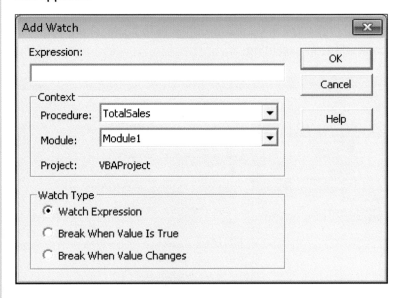

Type the name of the variable you want to monitor in the Expression box at the top and click OK. Doing so causes the Watches window to appear at the bottom of the Visual Basic Editor.

You can create as many watches as you want. Then, when you run your code, the Watches window displays the value of any variable for which you have set a watch. Because subroutines run very quickly, it's best to set breakpoints in your code so you can observe the values you're interested in at specific points in the routine.

To edit a watch, right-click it in the Watches window and click Edit Watch from the shortcut menu that appears to display the Edit Watch dialog box. The Edit Watch dialog box is identical, bar the name, to the Add Watch dialog box. To delete a watch, right-click it in the Watches window and click Delete Watch.

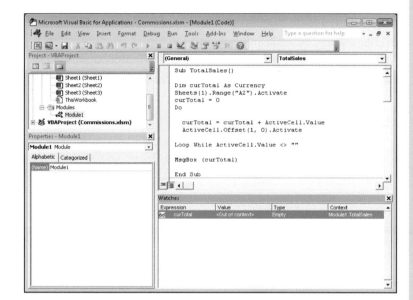

Did you know?

You can resize the Watches window by dragging its edges, just like other dialog boxes and panes in the Visual Basic Editor.

Step through your code one line at a time

Programming in VBA is an exacting process. The VBA interpreter does exactly what you tell it to, even if that's not what you meant for it to do. If your VBA code generates unexpected results and you are unable to discover the source of the error, you might need to step through your code one line at a time to identify the problem.

To execute one instruction at a time, press the F8 key. Doing so highlights the `Sub` statement at the top of the subroutine. When you press F8 again, the Visual Basic Editor executes the highlighted instruction and highlights the code on the next line.

Step through your code one line at a time

1 Display a subroutine.

2 Press F8 to execute the next line of code.

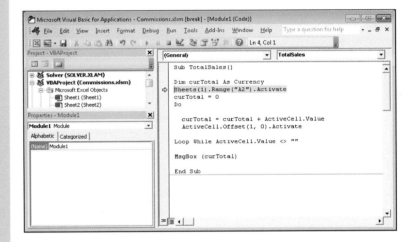

You can continue to execute your code in this way by pressing the F8 key. If you want to run your code to the end, press the F5 key.

Did you know?

Click **Run...Break** or press Ctrl+Break to stop executing the subroutine.

Did you know?

The Visual Basic Editor doesn't pause to highlight `Dim` statements.

Moving through your code one line at a time by pressing the F8 key is an extremely useful technique to help you identify problems in your code. Unfortunately, the process can be extremely slow for complicated routines or ones that contain loops which repeat numerous times.

If your VBA code calls a subroutine that you are certain returns a correct result, you can run the subroutine in its entirety and stop before executing the next line in the main subroutine. For example, suppose you want to call a subroutine that calculates commissions from another subroutine. The code for those two subroutines might look like this:

```
Sub CalculateCommission()

Dim curTotal As Currency

curTotal = ActiveCell.Value

MsgBox ("Sale value is £" & curTotal)

Select Case curTotal
Case Is >= 10000
    curCommission = curTotal * 0.08
Case Is >= 1000
    curCommission = curTotal * 0.06
Case Is >= 500
    curCommission = curTotal * 0.05
Case Else
    curCommission = curTotal * 0.04
End Select

MsgBox ("Your commission is £" &
curCommission)
End Sub
```

Skip over a subroutine

Skip over a subroutine
1 Press Shift+F8.

13

Skip over a subroutine (cont.)

The subroutine to call the commission calculator might look like this:

```
Sub DisplaySale()
Dim curSale As Currency

curSale = ActiveCell.Value
MsgBox ("Sale value is £" & curSale)
CalculateCommission
MsgBox ("Both routines completed.")
End Sub
```

If you place the cursor in the `DisplaySale` subroutine, pressing F8 will move you through its code one step at a time. When the line to call the `CalculateCommission` subroutine is highlighted, pressing Shift+F8 executes the entire called subroutine but halts before executing the line below it, in the `DisplaySale` subroutine.

> ### Did you know?
> Pressing Shift+F8 when the highlighted line of code doesn't call another subroutine has the same effect as pressing F8 – the Visual Basic Editor simply executes the next line of code.

As you become a more experienced VBA programmer, you will create code that calls one or more subroutines. When you debug your code, you'll often find it useful to move through the instructions step-by-step by pressing F8. For example, you could create code that uses a called subroutine to calculate sales commissions.

```
Sub DisplaySale()
Dim curSale As Currency

curSale = ActiveCell.Value
MsgBox ("Sale value is £" & curSale)
CalculateCommission (curSale)
End Sub
```

As you move through your code, you might find that, instead of skipping *over* a subroutine, you have pressed F8 and entered *into* the subroutine. If the highlighted instruction is within the subroutine and you would like to execute the rest of the subroutine without stopping, you can do so by pressing Control+Shift+ F8. When you do, the Visual Basic Editor will run the rest of the subroutine, halting only when it returns to the body of code that called subroutine.

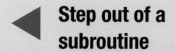

Did you know?

Pressing Control+Shift+F8 when the highlighted line of code isn't within a called subroutine has the same effect as pressing F8 – the Visual Basic Editor simply executes the next line of code.

Step out of a subroutine

Step out of a subroutine

1 Press Control+Shift+F8.

13

Manage errors using an `On Error GoTo` statement

Create an `On Error GoTo` statement

1. Create a subroutine.

2. In the body of the subroutine, do the following:

   a. Write a line of code such as `On Error GoTo label`:

   b. Write `Exit Sub` on the line above the line label.

   c. Write the line label, followed by a colon.

   d. Complete the error-handling code.

Writing Excel VBA routines can be a complicated process. As you become more familiar with the language and gain experience as a programmer, you will write increasingly complex code. This complexity all but guarantees you'll make some mistakes. There is also the very real possibility (even certainty) that your colleagues will make mistakes when interacting with your code. For example, you might ask them for a number representing a currency amount and they include the currency symbol or a comma when they shouldn't.

If someone enters a text string when your code expects a number, the Visual Basic Editor will exit the subroutine and display an error message.

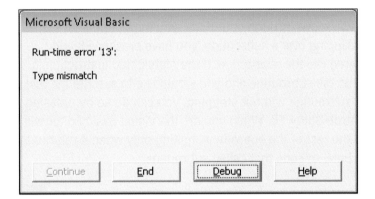

Rather than allow your macro to come to a crashing halt, you can add code to a subroutine to handle these errors more gracefully. One way to do that is to include an `On Error GoTo` statement. This statement has two components. The first is the `On Error GoTo` statement itself, which identifies the line of code the subroutine should jump to when an error occurs. The second part is a line label, followed by a colon, that corresponds to the label in the `On Error GoTo`. For example, you could have the line label `Handler:` identify your error-handling code:

```
Sub CheckError()
Dim lngNumber As Long
On Error GoTo Handler:
lngNumber = InputBox("Enter a number.")
MsgBox (lngNumber)
Exit Sub
Handler:
MsgBox ("Enter the number without
currency symbols or commas.")
End Sub
```

In most cases, error-handling code appears at the end of the subroutine with an **Exit Sub** line just above the line label. If you missed out the **Exit Sub** statement, which causes the Visual Basic Editor to stop executing subroutine's code, the subroutine would run the error-handling code even though it's not needed.

If the user enters a text string into the input box created in the subroutine, Excel would display the message box defined within the error-handling code.

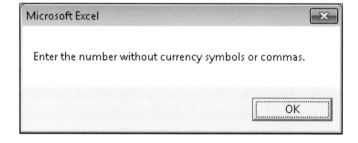

Manage errors using an On Error Resume Next statement

Manage errors using an On Error Resume Next statement

1 Create a subroutine.

2 In the body of the subroutine, type **On Error Resume Next** on its own line.

Important

If you type the **On Error Resume Next** statement below the code to be executed, the Visual Basic Editor uses the default error-handling mode (showing dialog boxes describing the error) until it encounters the **On Error Resume Next** statement.

Handling errors in your VBA code can be difficult, especially early on in the programming process when you're not certain everything is working correctly and it's hard to identify their causes. If you want the Visual Basic Editor to continue to execute your code even though it has encountered an error, you can use the **On Error Resume Next** statement. If you put the statement at the top of a subroutine, the editor will ignore any errors and continue to run your code, starting with the line after the line that caused the error.

```
Sub CheckError()
Dim lngNumber As Long
On Error Resume Next
lngNumber = InputBox("Enter a number.")
MsgBox (lngNumber)
End Sub
```

Using the **On Error Resume Next** statement might seem like an easy way to ensure that all of the code after the error is running correctly, but you should be aware that errors tend to cascade. If the offending instruction provides a value that's used later on in your code, you won't get a true test of your code's accuracy.

Running the above subroutine and typing the letter 'a' into the input box causes Excel to display a message box that contains the number zero. The message box contains a zero because the letter 'a' is not an acceptable value for variables of type **Long**, but the **On Error Resume Next** statement has turned off error messages. Therefore, Excel displays the value zero, which represents no value or, as in this case, a non-numerical value.

You can change the default Visual Basic editor error-handling behaviour using one of two statements: `On Error GoTo` or `On Error Resume Next`. If you have implemented either of those methods at the start of your code module, but want to change back to the Visual Basic Editor's *default* error-handling mode, you can do so using the statement `On Error GoTo 0`.

The benefit of switching back to the default error-handling mode, which halts code execution and displays an error message, is that you can start by implementing error handling for a portion of your code where potential errors are reasonably well-defined. Then, when you get to a portion of your code in which you have less confidence, you can switch back to the default error-handling mode and have Excel display error messages and highlight the offending line of code so you have a better chance of discovering and fixing the error.

Did you know?

If you want to use Excel's default error-handling mode, you don't need to add the `On Error GoTo 0` line to your subroutine – the Visual Basic Editor will use that mode automatically.

◀ **Manage errors using an `On Error GoTo 0` statement**

Manage errors using an `On Error GoTo 0` statement

1. Create a subroutine.

2. In the body of the subroutine, type `On Error GoTo 0` on its own line.

13

Using Excel events in your VBA code

Introduction

Excel VBA gives you a great deal of control over your workbook. You can also use events to determine what actions, if any, Excel takes when your colleagues undertake specific actions. For example, you might want to verify that your colleague really wants to close a workbook if certain information has been entered into it.

The subroutines described in this chapter all use the private keyword at the beginning of the Sub declaration. Doing so limits the event handler's scope to the current workbook, which has the benefit of preventing any other open workbooks from running the code when you don't want them to.

What you'll do

Display the available events

Run a procedure when you open a workbook

Run a procedure when you close a workbook

Run a procedure when you save a workbook

Run a procedure when a cell range changes

Display the available events

In the Excel 2010 object-oriented programming model, Excel objects have three different types of attributes: properties, methods and events. A property is some aspect of an object, such as the object's name. A method is something the object can do, such as print or export its values to a text file. An event is an action the object recognises, such as changing the value in a cell or a user clicking a hyperlink. Almost every Excel object has one or more events associated with it.

In the Object Browser, events are indicated by a yellow lightning bolt. When you click an event, its description appears at the bottom of the Object Browser.

Display the available events

1. If necessary, in the Visual Basic Editor, click View, then Object Browser on the menu bar to display the Object Browser.

2. To limit the classes displayed, click the Project/Library control's down arrow and click Excel.

3. Click the object for which you want to view available events in the Classes panel to display the properties, methods and events for that class.

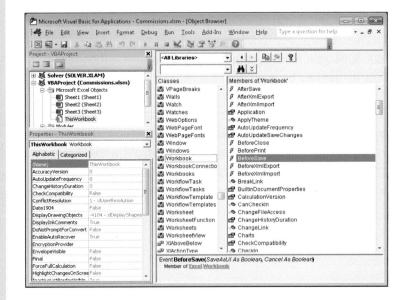

?

Did you know?

Alternatively, you can press F2 to display the Object Browser.

?

Did you know?

To display the Help file associated with an event, click the event and then click the Help button, which has a question mark on its face.

Previously, when you created a VBA subroutine or function, you did so by inserting a code module into your workbook's VBA project. These code modules are available from anywhere within your workbook or any other open workbook if the routines are public. Events, on the other hand, are tied directly to specific workbook objects, such as worksheets or even the workbook itself.

If you want to run a specific subroutine when your workbook is opened, you need to open the code module that is tied directly to the workbook. To do that, you double-click the ThisWorkbook item in the Project Explorer. If the Project Explorer isn't currently open, you can display it by clicking View, then Project Explorer on the menu bar.

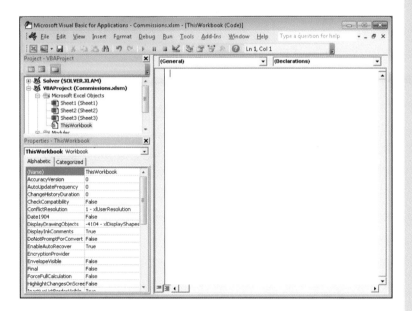

When you double-click the ThisWorkbook item, the Visual Basic Editor opens the code module associated with the workbook. You can then create subroutines that run whenever a given event occurs. For example, if you want to run a routine whenever the workbook is opened, you would use the following code structure:

 Run a procedure when you open a workbook

Run a procedure when you open a workbook

1 In the project window, double-click the ThisWorkbook item.

2 Create a subroutine that starts with the statement `Private Sub Workbook_Open ()`.

3 Type the code to be run when the workbook opens between the `Sub` and `End Sub` statements.

14

Run a procedure when you open a workbook (cont.)

```
Private Sub Workbook_Open()
MsgBox ("This workbook contains
commission data.")
End Sub
```

Note that the **Sub** declaration at the top of the subroutine has the word **Sub** followed by the object named **Workbook**, then an underscore, then the name of the event that triggers the code. The example above displays a message box whenever the workbook is opened.

Did you know?

To display the Project Explorer by using a keyboard shortcut, press Ctrl+R .

Important

You may only have one subroutine triggered by a specific event per workbook, but you may have multiple actions within the event code.

If you work in a business, you probably manage confidential data, such as salary or sales information. If your corporate compliance practices require that you remind your employees of data sensitivity whenever they close a workbook, you can do so by attaching code to the **Workbook** object's **BeforeClose** event.

To do that, you double-click the ThisWorkbook item in the Project Explorer. If the Project Explorer isn't currently open, you can display it by clicking View, then Project Explorer on the menu bar. Then, in the code space that appears, type a routine that follows this pattern:

```
Private Sub Workbook_BeforeClose(Cancel
As Boolean)
MsgBox ("Remember the data is
confidential.")
Answer = MsgBox("Do you really want to
close the workbook?", vbYesNo)
If Answer = vbNo Then Cancel = True
End Sub
```

Note that the **Sub** declaration statement is a bit different than that used for the **Open** event. The **Private Sub** keywords lead off the line, followed by the name of the object, in this case **Workbook**, then an underscore character and the name of the event. That information is followed by the words **Cancel As Boolean** in parentheses. The phrase **Cancel as Boolean** appears at the end of the event code **Sub** declaration so the routine can detect whether the close operation has been cancelled or not. If it has, then the code either won't run at all or won't run again as a result of the triggering action that just occurred. This code displays a message box asking if the user truly wishes to close the workbook. If not, they can click No to cancel the operation.

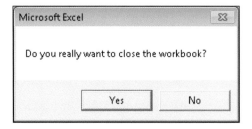

Run a procedure when you close a workbook

1. In the Project Explorer window, double-click the ThisWorkbook item.

2. Create a subroutine that starts with the statement **Private Sub Workbook_ BeforeClose (Cancel as Boolean)**.

3. Type the code to be run before the workbook closes between the **Sub** and **End Sub** statements.

14

?

Did you know?

If your **BeforeClose** event code changes the contents of your workbook, you won't be able to review the changes before the workbook closes.

Run a procedure when you save a workbook

Run a procedure when you save a workbook

1. In the project window, double-click the ThisWorkbook item.

2. Create a subroutine that starts with the statement **Private Sub Workbook_BeforeSave (ByVal SaveAsUI as Boolean, Cancel as Boolean)**.

3. Type the code to be run before the workbook closes between the **Sub** and **End Sub** statements.

Saving a workbook is rarely a controversial act. In most cases, you should encourage your colleagues to save their data as frequently as is practical. Even so, there might be occasions where you want to verify if a user really wants to save their data. For example, an accountant might keep a strict log of every change made to every workbook. If that's the case, then saving the workbook commits those changes to the archive. Again, it's not an unexpected result, but it might be something that you, as a programmer, wish to bring to your colleagues' attention.

To create code using the **Workbook_BeforeSave** event, use the following template:

```
Private Sub Workbook_BeforeSave(ByVal
SaveAsUI as Boolean,Cancel as Boolean)
Answer = MsgBox("Are you sure you want
to save your data?", vbYesNo)
If Answer = vbNo Then Cancel = True
End Sub
```

The **Sub** declaration accepts two parameters, passed by value. The first is **SaveAsUI**, which indicates whether or not Excel should display the SaveAs dialog box. This action might occur if the user is saving the workbook for the first time. The **Cancel** argument has the same role as in the **BeforeClose** event. You can ask if the user truly wishes to save the workbook. If so, they can click the Yes button to complete the operation.

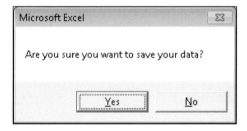

The event procedures described earlier in this chapter are all triggered by events at the *workbook* level. You can also create procedures that are triggered by events at the *worksheet* level. To create an event procedure triggered by a change in the worksheet, you open the Project Explorer and then double-click the worksheet you want to use to open a code module for that worksheet. As an example, you could create event-handling routines for the worksheet named Sheet1.

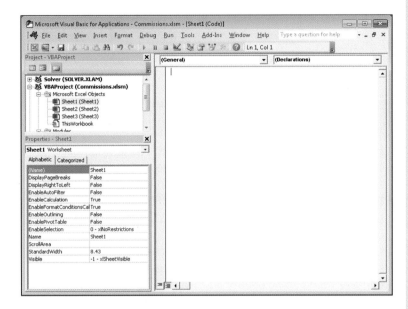

One of the most common events you will use at the worksheet level is the **Change** event. This triggers whenever a substantive change is made to a worksheet. For example, you might wish to keep a record of all edits made to a worksheet. You create a **Change** event using code that follows this structure:

```
Private Sub Worksheet_Change (ByVal
Target As Excel.Range)
  MsgBox("The cell range " & Target.
Address & " was updated.")
End Sub
```

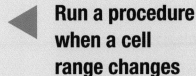

Run a procedure when a cell range changes

Run a procedure when a cell range changes

1. In the Project Window, double-click the item representing the worksheet to which you want to assign the event.

2. Type the first line of the event code as **Private Sub Worksheet_Change (ByVal Target As Excel.Range)**.

3. Between the **Sub** and **End Sub** lines of code, enter the instructions you want executed when a cell range changes on that worksheet.

14

Run a procedure when a cell range changes (cont.)

The code within the body of the subroutine could be anything. In this case, the code simply shows the address of the cell range that was changed.

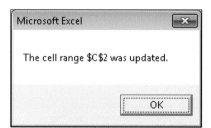

Gathering data with UserForms

Introduction

Many Excel users take pride in the worksheets and workbooks they develop, and rightfully so. The most effective solutions combine data entry and presentation seamlessly, letting users do their work in the shortest time possible so they can get on with other tasks. Even solutions that fail to reach this status can be exceptionally useful for the designer and his or her colleagues.

From a data entry standpoint, though, very little compares to the effectiveness of `UserForms`. A `UserForm`, which you create in the Visual Basic Editor, provides a simple interface for data entry. Among the many possibilities open to you are that you can allow users to enter any data they wish into a `TextBox`, restrict their entries to those presented in a `ListBox` or combine the two approaches in a `ComboBox`. You can select the best approach for an application and implement it quickly.

Here, you will learn how to create a `UserForm`, add controls to it, write `UserForm` data to a worksheet and manage the `UserForm`.

What you'll do

Create a `UserForm`

Add a `TextBox` **to a** `UserForm`

Add a `ListBox` **to a** `UserForm`

Add a `ComboBox` **to a** `UserForm`

Add an option button to a `UserForm`

Add graphics to a `UserForm`

Add a `SpinButton` **to a** `UserForm`

Create a multipage or multitab `UserForm`

Write `UserForm` **data to a worksheet**

Display, load and hide a `UserForm`

Create a
UserForm

Create a UserForm

1 In the Visual Basic Editor, click Insert, then UserForm on the menu bar.

2 If desired, edit the **UserForm's Name** property to change the name you use to refer to it in your code.

3 If desired, edit the **UserForm's Caption** property to change the caption that appears on the **UserForm's** title bar.

Important

A **UserForm's** name must start with a letter and may only contain letters, numbers and the underscore character.

So far in this guide, you have created code modules to store your VBA code. When you create a **UserForm**, you also create an underlying code module that contains the subroutines that define the **UserForm** objects' behaviours.

To create a **UserForm**, press Alt+F11 to display the Visual Basic Editor, then click Insert, then UserForm on the menu bar to create a blank **UserForm**.

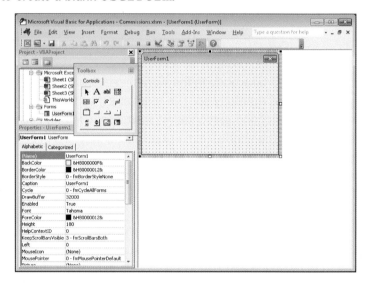

A **UserForm** is like any other Excel object, so you can change its size by dragging any of the handles on its sides or corners. Dragging a handle in the middle of a side changes the **UserForm's** height or width, while dragging a handle at a **UserForm's** corner changes both height and width.

By default, your **UserForm** has a name such as **UserForm1**, representing the **UserForm's** place in the **UserForms** collection. You can change a **UserForm's** name by editing its **Name** property. The **Name** property is the internal representation of the **UserForm** (that is, how you will refer to it in your code), so you should consider putting the letters '*frm*' at the start of the name to indicate that it represents 'a form'.

The word or words that appear on a **UserForm's** title bar are controlled by the **Caption** property. To change the **UserForm's** caption, click the **UserForm** and then, in the Properties panel, click the box next to the **Caption** property and edit its value.

With the **UserForm** in place, you can now add controls and the code to power them within your Excel workbook.

One of the most useful capabilities you can offer on a **UserForm** is that of being able to type their name, address or other information into a control. In Excel VBA, that control is the **TextBox**. To add a **TextBox** to a **UserForm**, display the Toolbox, click the **TextBox** button, then, in the body of the **UserForm**, drag to define the textbox. After you create the **TextBox**, a list of its properties appears in the Properties panel.

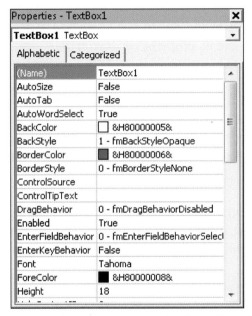

There are a number of properties you might want to edit. The first is the **Name** property, which appears at the top of the list as (Name). You should change the control's name to reflect the data it will contain. For example, you could assign the name **Cust_ First_Name** to a **TextBox** meant to accept a customer's first name. The control's name must start with a letter and may contain only letters, numbers and underscore characters.

You can also add a label to identify the control and indicate the data to be entered. To add a label, display the Toolbox, click the Label button and drag to define the label in the body of the form. Position the label so it's in line with the **TextBox** and then change the label's **Caption** property so it contains the text required to identify its related control.

Add a **TextBox** to a **UserForm**

Add a **TextBox** to a **UserForm**

1 Open a **UserForm** and then, in the Toolbox, click the TextBox button.

2 Drag on to the body of the **UserForm** to define the **TextBox**.

3 If desired, change the **TextBox**'s **Name** property to change the name by which you refer to the **TextBox** in your code.

4 If desired, create a label, edit the label's **Caption** property to change the text it displays and position the label next to the **TextBox**.

Important

A control's name may not be a reserved word, such as 'Variant' or 'Sub'.

15

Add a ListBox to a UserForm

Add a ListBox to a UserForm

1 Open a UserForm and then, in the Toolbox, click the ListBox button.

2 Drag on to the body of the UserForm to define the ListBox.

3 Define an Excel table and type =*tablename* in the ListBox's RowSource property box.

4 If desired, change the Listbox's Name property to change the name by which you refer to the ListBox in your code.

5 If desired, create a label, edit the label's Caption property to change the text it displays, then position the label next to the ListBox.

A TextBox, described elsewhere in this chapter, lets a user enter text into the control without restriction. Entering text with no guidelines is useful, but it also opens up the possibility of multiple spellings or misspellings for the same term. By contrast, a ListBox requires a user to select a value from a predetermined list. ListBoxes increase data entry accuracy at the expense of user flexibility.

To create a ListBox, display a UserForm in the Visual Basic Editor, display the Toolbox, click the ListBox button, then drag to within the body of the UserForm to define the ListBox. When you do, the ListBox appears on the UserForm and its properties appear in the Properties panel on the left side of the Visual Basic Editor window.

A ListBox control draws its values from a range of worksheet cells. To assign a cell range to a ListBox, you enter the range's definition into the ListBox's RowSource property. In Excel 2010, the easiest way to define the row source for a ListBox is to create a one-column Excel table. To create an Excel table, create a data list with a header in a worksheet and then, on the Home tab of the ribbon, click the Format as Table button and click the desired table style. Doing so displays the Format As Table dialog box.

Verify that the My table has headers box is selected and then click 'OK' to create the table. With the table still selected, on the Design contextual tab of the ribbon, type a new name for your table in the Table Name box. For example, if your ListBox presents a list of countries in the world, you could simply name your table 'Countries'.

With your data source defined, you can now type in equals sign followed by the name of the table in the **RowSource** property for your **ListBox**. Now when you run the **UserForm** and click the down arrow at the right edge of the **ListBox**, you will be able to select a country from the list.

Did you know?

Excel tables were introduced in Excel 2007.

Did you know?

When you add or delete an Excel table row, the program updates its internal reference to the data, so you don't have to update the **RowSource** property's contents to reflect the change.

Add a ListBox to a UserForm (cont.)

15

Add a
ComboBox to a UserForm

Add a ComboBox to a UserForm

1 Open a UserForm and then, in the Toolbox, click the ComboBox button.

2 Drag it onto the body of the UserForm to define the ComboBox.

3 Define an Excel table and type =*tablename* in the ComboBox's RowSource property box.

4 If desired, change the ComboBox's Name property to change the name by which you refer to the ComboBox in your code.

5 If desired, create a label, edit the label's Caption property to change the text it displays and position the label next to the ComboBox.

A ListBox, described earlier in this chapter, lets a user select a value from a predetermined list of values. A ComboBox is similar, with one significant difference: the user can also type their own value into the control. A ComboBox offers more flexibility than a ListBox, but it also introduces the possibility that misspellings might cause the same value to be entered in several different ways.

To add a ComboBox to a UserForm, display a UserForm in the Visual Basic Editor and then, in the Toolbox, click the ComboBox button. Draw the outline of the ComboBox on the body of the UserForm and, when you release the left mouse button, the ComboBox control appears and its properties appear in the Properties panel on the left side of the Visual Basic Editor.

As with a ListBox, the most flexible way to provide values for a ComboBox in Excel 2010 is to define an Excel table. For example, you might create a form for user feedback and allow the user to select from four different categories to enter their own. To assign an Excel table named 'Categories' to a ComboBox, click the ComboBox and then set its Row Source property to the value =Categories. Now when the user clicks the ComboBox's down arrow those values will appear, but the user will also have the option of typing their own value into the box.

See also

For more information on creating and renaming in Excel table, see the Add a ListBox to a UserForm task earlier in this chapter.

`ListBoxes`, `ComboBoxes` and `TextBoxes` are terrific tools that let users enter or select numerous values. If the users' choice is more constrained, you can let them indicate their choice by selecting or clearing option buttons. Option buttons let users indicate whether an option, such as to gift wrap a purchase or not, is turned on or turned off. You can also create groups of option buttons that let a users select, at most, one option from the group at a time.

You can change the option button's appearance and behaviour using the properties available to you, but the most common properties you'll change are the button's **Name** and **Caption** properties.

The **Name** property controls how the option button is referenced within the `UserForm` and your VBA code. Changing it makes your references more readable but doesn't change the text displayed next to the option button in the `UserForm`. To change that text, you need to change the value of the **Caption** property. For example, you could change the **Caption** property to read 'Gift wrapped'.

You can also create groups of option buttons where only one of the buttons can be selected at a time. For example, you might want a user to select a shipping method from among the options of ground, two day and overnight. To allow only one option button of those three to be selected at a time, you must assign the same value to each button's **GroupName** property. For example, you could create the Shipping group to allow only one selection from several shipping alternatives.

Add an option button to a `UserForm`

Add an option button to a `UserForm`

1. Open a `UserForm` in the Visual Basic Editor and then, in the Toolbox, click the OptionButton button.

2. Click in the body of the `UserForm` where you want the button to appear to create it and display its properties in the Properties panel.

3. If desired, change the `ComboBox`'s **Name** property to change the name by which you refer to the option button in your code.

4. If desired, edit the option button's **Caption** property to change the text it displays.

5. If desired, assign a value to the **GroupName** property. Only one option button among those that share the same **GroupName** property value can be selected at one time.

15

Add an option button to a `UserForm` (cont.)

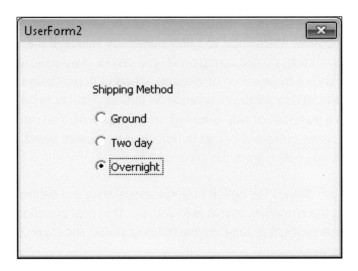

`UserForms` are powerful objects, but you have relatively little control over their appearance, especially compared to the wide variety of formatting options you have for a worksheet and the objects within it. One way to add some visual interest or useful information to a VBA `UserForm` is by adding images.

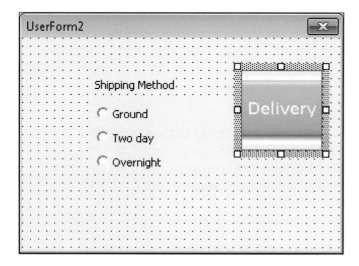

Unless the image you select fits entirely within the frame, you will likely see just a portion of it on the `UserForm`. You can control the way the image fits within the frame by changing the `PictureSizeMode` property. That property has three possible values:

1 0 – `fmPictureSizeModeClip` displays as much of the image as possible within the frame.

2 1 – `fmPictureSizeModeStretch` displays the entire image within the frame, but stretches the image so it fills the entire frame.

3 3 – `fmPictureSizeModeZoom` displays the entire image within the frame, but keeps the vertical and horizontal dimensions in their original ratio.

 Add graphics to a `UserForm`

Add graphics to a `UserForm`

1 Open a `UserForm` in the Visual Basic Editor, then, in the Toolbox, click the Image button.

2 Drag within the body of the `UserForm` to create the image frame. When you release the left mouse button, the image frame will appear.

3 In the Properties panel, the image control's properties will appear. Click in the box next to the `Picture` property name.

4 Click the Browse button that appears, select the desired image, then click Open. The image appears on the `UserForm`.

5 Change the value of the `PictureSizeMode` property so your image displays correctly.

15

Add graphics to a `UserForm` (cont)

?

Did you know?

You can change the name of the image control, which is the label by which you refer to the image in your VBA code, by editing the control's `Name` property.

?

Did you know?

If you set the `PictureSizeMode` property to `fmPictureSizeModeStretch` or `fmPictureSizeModeZoom`, changing the size of the image frame also changes the size of the image displayed within it.

Excel VBA **UserForms** let you and your colleagues enter data into your spreadsheets efficiently. **TextBoxes** provide the most flexibility, but they also allow users to make mistakes. If you want more control over the numbers a user enters, you can attach a **SpinButton** control to a **TextBox** or label. Clicking the **SpinButton**'s up or down arrow changes the value in the attached control by an increment you define.

There are three steps to implementing a **SpinButton** in your **UserForm**. The first of these is to create the **SpinButton** itself, which you can do by clicking the **UserForm** and then, in the Toolbox, clicking the **SpinButton** control and dragging the **SpinButton** on to the body of the **UserForm**. You can now define the value range and increment that each click of an up or down arrow will change the value of the **SpinButton** by. To do that, click the **SpinButton** and then, in the Properties panel, change the values of the **Max**, **Min** and **SmallChange** properties. **Min** is the smallest value that can be assigned to the **SpinButton**, **Max** is the largest value and **SmallChange** is the increment that each click will change the value by. For example, if you set a **Min** of 20, a **Max** of 200 and **SmallChange** of 10, you could select the values 20, 30, 40, 50 and so on in increments of 10 all the way up to 200.

With the **SpinButton** in place, you should use techniques shown earlier in this chapter to create a **TextBox** that displays the value assigned to the **SpinButton** control. Make a note of the name of the **TextBox**, which you can discover by clicking it and observing the value of the **Name** property in the Properties panel. You will need to know the name to create the code used to link the **SpinButton** with that **TextBox**.

Right-click the **SpinButton** and, from the shortcut menu that appears, click View Code. Doing so displays the outline of the event code that will run when the value of the **SpinButton** changes. To link the **SpinButton** with the **TextBox**, you set the text control's **Value** property so it is equal to the same property of the **SpinButton**.

Add a SpinButton to a UserForm

Add a SpinButton to a UserForm

1. Open a **UserForm** and then, in the Toolbox, click the **SpinButton** control.

2. Drag the **SpinButton** onto the **UserForm**.

3. Create a **TextBox**.

4. Right-click the **SpinButton** and click View Code from the shortcut menu.

5. Create an event handler that assigns the value of the **SpinButton** to the **TextBox**.

15

Add a SpinButton to a UserForm (cont)

If the `TextBox` were named `SpinValue` and the `SpinButton` were named `SpinButton1`, your code would look like this:

```
Private Sub SpinButton1_Change()
  SpinValue.Value = SpinButton1.Value
End Sub
```

Did you know?

Changing the `Name` property for the `SpinButton` and `TextBox` can make it easier for you and your colleagues to understand the code you create to link the two controls.

Before you create a `UserForm`, you should take the time to sketch out its design using pencil and paper. The more you think about the data you want to capture with it and how you can facilitate that process, the more time you save when you create it in Excel.

If you find that you can't fit all of the controls you need on a single `UserForm` page, you have options. You can create a multipage `UserForm` or multitab one.

By default, a multipage `UserForm` has two pages. You can add, delete, rename and move pages within it by right-clicking any tab at the top of the page. Doing so displays a shortcut menu with the available options.

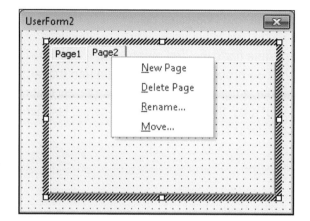

You can add, delete, rename and move tabs in a multitab `UserForm` in exactly the same manner as you would pages in a multipage `UserForm`.

Did you know?
The contents of the Properties panel reflect the active page in the multipage `UserForm`.

Did you know?
Some designers create prototypes of their user interfaces in PowerPoint, using the shapes and lines available in that program.

Create a multipage or multitab `UserForm`

Create a multipage or multitab `UserForm`

1 Open a `UserForm` and then, in the Toolbox, click the MultiPage button to create a multipage `UserForm`.

  a. Drag it on to the `UserForm` to define the `MultiPage` control.

  b. Add controls to the page using techniques shown elsewhere in this chapter.

  c. Use the shortcut menu, accessed by right-clicking a tab, to add, rename, move and delete pages as desired.

2 Open a `UserForm` and then, in the Toolbox, click the TabStrip button to create a multitab `UserForm`.

  a. Drag it on to the `UserForm` to define the `TabStrip` control.

  b. Add controls to the page using techniques shown elsewhere in this chapter.

  c. Use the shortcut menu, accessed by right-clicking a tab, to add, rename, move and delete pages as desired.

15

Write
UserForm data to a worksheet

After you've created your **UserForm**, you need to create code that will write the values from the **UserForm** to a worksheet. You do that by adding a command button to your form and adding code to the button's **On_Click** event that will read the value of every control on the form and write them to the appropriate worksheet cells.

The process for reading and writing these values involves two major steps. The first step is to find the first empty row in the target worksheet. For example, if your data list already contains three rows, you don't want the current input to overwrite any of the existing data. To avoid that problem, the code starts at the bottom of the worksheet and searches for the first completed cell in a column where you want to write your data. The routine then targets the row *below* that cell.

After the routine finds the first empty row, it uses the **Cells** object's **Value** property to write the data into the target cells. As an example, suppose you have a **UserForm** that collects four pieces of data: the customer's first name, last name, country and status as a new customer.

CustomerEntry	✕
First Name	
Last Name	
Country	
◯ New customer?	

You now should create a command button to which you can attach code that writes the values to the worksheet. To create the command button, display a **UserForm** and then, in the Toolbox, click the CommandButton control. Drag the button on to the **UserForm** and, if desired, change the button's `Caption` property so the text that appears on the button is easier for you and your colleagues to understand.

Right-click the button and, from the shortcut menu that appears, click View Code to display the button's `On_Click` event-handling code. You could use the following routine to find the first empty cell in column A of your worksheet, read the values in the four controls, then write values into the worksheet:

```
Private Sub CommandButton1_Click()
Dim lngEntryRow As Long

Worksheets("Sheet1").Activate
lngEntryRow = Worksheets("Sheet1").
Range("A1048576").End(xlUp).Row + 1

Cells(lngEntryRow, 1) = Cust_FirstName.
Value
Cells(lngEntryRow, 2) = Cust_LastName.
Value
Cells(lngEntryRow, 3) = Cust_Country.
Value
Cells(lngEntryRow, 4) = opt_NewStatus.
Value
Cells(lngEntryRow, 4).Activate
End Sub
```

If there were already three records in the target worksheet, entering data from the **UserForm** would result in the following list.

	A	B	C	D	E
1	**FirstName**	**LastName**	**Country**	**NewStatus**	
2	Arthur	Kondrake	USA	FALSE	
3	Olivier	Martin	France	TRUE	
4	Martine	Chatras	Belgium	FALSE	
5	Curtis	Frye	USA	TRUE	
6					
7					

Write UserForm data to a worksheet (cont.)

Write UserForm data to a worksheet

1 On the **UserForm**, create a command button.

2 Right-click the command button and click View Code.

3 Write code that finds the first empty cell below the target data list.

4 Write code that writes each control's value to the appropriate cell in the row.

15

? Did you know?

Excel 2007 and Excel 2010 worksheets contain 1,048,576 rows.

Display, load and hide a UserForm

Display, load and hide a UserForm

1 Invoke the `UserForm.Show` method.

2 Invoke the `UserForm.Load` method.

3 Invoke the `UserForm.Hide` method.

See also

For more information on running a macro by clicking a worksheet shape, see Chapter 1.

Did you know?

Loading a `UserForm` decreases the time it takes it to appear when you invoke the `Show` method.

Once you define a `UserForm` in your VBA code, you need to display it so the user can interact with it. The Excel VBA code to display a `UserForm` is quite straightforward. As an example, suppose you have a form named `frmCustomerEntry`. All you need to do is type the name of the form followed by a full stop and the `Show` method. For example, the code to display `frmCustomerEntry` would be:

```
frmCustomerEntry.Show
```

You can test a `UserForm` from within the Visual Basic Editor by displaying the `UserForm` and then either clicking Run, then Run Sub/UserForm on the menu system or by pressing the F5 key.

You can also enter a `UserForm` into the application's memory without displaying it. To do that, you use the `Load` method. The command to load the same form into the Excel program's memory would be:

```
frmCustomerEntry.Load
```

When you later want to display the `UserForm` in Excel, you can call the `Show` method in the way noted earlier.

Hiding a `UserForm`, as you might expect, relies on the `Hide` method. The syntax looks exactly the same as it does for the `Show` and `Load` methods:

```
frmCustomerEntry.Hide
```

The most common way to invoke the `Hide` method is to create a command button with the label 'Cancel' and run the `Hide` method when a user clicks that button. *Users* can also hide a `UserForm` by clicking the 'Close' box at the top right corner of the `UserForm`.

Jargon buster

Absolute reference An instruction that identifies a specific cell range and doesn't change when the reference is copied to another cell.

Active cell The cell that is highlighted in a worksheet.

Active region A rectangle of cells that extends from the active cell to the top and bottom rows and left- and right-most columns of cells that are connected to the active cell.

Alert A message box indicating the consequences of an action.

Argument A value used by a function.

Array A construct that can contain multiple examples of a data type.

Breakpoint A user-defined line in a code module where the Visual Basic Editor halts code execution.

Bug A programming error.

Chart sheet A sheet designed to hold a single chart (as opposed to a worksheet, which can contain charts, data and other objects).

Code A generic term for instructions in a programming language.

Collection A set of all objects of a type (e.g., the Worksheets collection).

Comment In Visual Basic for Applications, a non-executable line of code used to provide information about a procedure.

Condition A test used to determine whether subsequent code should be executed.

Constant A variable that doesn't change value during code execution.

Custom list A user-defined set of values used in sorting operations.

Data series A set of related data depicted in a chart.

Data type The characteristic of a variable that determines what data it can contain.

Debugging The art of identifying and fixing programming errors.

Default The value or behaviour a program component takes on if you don't change it.

Delimiter A character that identifies the end of one value and the beginning of the next in a text file.

Digital signature A file, generated by a certification authority, that Excel can use to identify a document as having been created by the certificate owner.

Dot notation A method for identifying components of objects, such as properties, methods, and events.

Event An object attribute that lets the object respond when it is acted upon in a specific way.

Export To send data from one construct (such as a code module) to another (such as a text file).

Field A column in a data list or database table.

Filter A construct that limits the data shown in a worksheet.

Function A block of code that returns the result of a calculation.

Hide To remove a workbook element, such as a worksheet or column, from active display within the workbook without deleting the element.

Keyboard shortcut (also shortcut key) A sequence of keys that trigger a specific action, such as running a macro.

Loop A section of Visual Basic for Applications code that can be repeated.

Macro A named block of Visual Basic for Applications code.

Method An object attribute that takes an action affecting the object.

Module A collection of Visual Basic for Applications code routines.

Named range A cell range to which the user has assigned a name for easy reference.

Object variable A data container that represents an Excel object such as a workbook or worksheet.

Object-orientated programming A method of organising computer instructions where the things manipulated by the code are represented as objects with attributes.

Operator A mathematical symbol representing an action or comparison (e.g., + or >=)

Parameter A value used by a command.

Path A string representing the physical location of a file.

Point 1/72 of an inch (used to identify font sizes)

Print area The cell range (or ranges) that will be printed when a user prints the worksheet.

Procedure A named sequence of statements.

Project A set of code modules.

Property An object attribute that describes one aspect of the object.

Range A group of one or more cells.

Relative reference An instruction that tells Excel to look a number of rows up or down and a number of columns to the left or right of another cell.

Reserved word A term, such as Date or Integer, that may not be used as a variable or procedure name.

RGB A colour value system used to describe colours as a mixture of red (R), green (G), and blue (B). Each colour is represented with an integer in the range from 0 (colour is not present) to 255 (full intensity).

Run To execute a block of code.

Scope The degree to which other procedures and code modules can interact with a variable or procedure.

Sort To rearrange data according to one or more criteria.

Sparkline A word-sized graphic summarising data (invented by Edward Tufte).

Static variable A variable that does not lose its value when its procedure terminates.

Subroutine A block of code that affects a workbook but does not return a value that can be used in a formula.

Syntax The grammar of a programming language.

Transpose To reorder data by making rows into columns and columns into rows.

UserForm A custom interface for data entry and viewing.

Variable A named container that can store data.

Visual Basic Editor The environment in which you can create and modify Visual Basic for Applications code.

Troubleshooting guide

Working with data and variables

Managing workbooks and files

Formatting worksheets and worksheet elements

Sorting and filtering data